ANTI-INFLAMMATORY DIET COOKBOOK FOR BEGINNERS

A Quick and Easy Collection of Healthy Recipes to Lose Weight, Detoxify Your Body, Improve Immunity, and Beat Chronic Inflammation

Veronica Kelley

TABLE OF CONTENTS

ANTI-INFLAMMATORY DIET GUIDE 7

CHAPTER 1: INFLAMMATION AND ANTI-INFLAMMATORY DIET 8

What Are the Causes of Inflammation? 8

Mini Guide on How to Behave and Avoid Risk Factors 8

The Importance of Diet to Fight Inflammation..9

What Are the Foods to Avoid Drastically...9

Foods That Should Not Be Missing in an Anti-Inflammatory Diet.....................9

Inflammation, Intolerances, and Allergies...10

CHAPTER 2: THE BEST ANTI-INFLAMMATORY SUPPLEMENTS 11

Curcumin..11

Ginger 11

Spirulina...11

Vitamin D...12

Bromelain...12

CHAPTER 3: RECIPES 13

Breakfast Recipes...13

1. Apricot, Pistachio, and Cinnamon Yogurt Bowl 13

2. Avocado, Vanilla, and Chocolate Toast...14

3. Banana and Kiwi Milkshake 15

4. Cabbage and Jalapeno Frittata 16

5. Cucumber and Strawberry Toast..17

6. Ginger and Avocado Pancakes 18

7. Mango, Almonds, and Egg Toast...19

8. Peanuts, Coconut, and Ginger Muffins 20

9. Spicy Pecan Cookies 21

10. Turkey and Cumin Scrambled Egg Toast 22

Appetizers 23

11. Beetroot and Ginger Eggs 23

12. Carrot and Soy Cheese-Filled Lettuce 25

13. Soy Cheese and Papaya Dish 26

14. Orange and Chili Avocado 27

15. Papaya and Cherry Fruit Salad 28

16. Peas, Avocado, and Garlic Cream 29

17. Soy Cheese and Fruit Bowl 30

18. Pumpkin, Almond, and Cumin Flan 31

19. Tuna and Honey-Stuffed Pumpkin 32

20. Zucchini and Tomato Sandwich 33

First-Course Dishes 34

21. Pasta with Chicken, Asparagus, and Leeks 34

22. Avocado and Turkey Cream 36

23. Chipotle Chicken and Bean Soup 37

24. Cabbage and Scallop Rice 38

25. Chickpea, Tuna, and Dill Soup 39

26. Cod, Pine Nuts, and Quinoa Curry 40

27. Spicy Kale Cream 41

28. Rice and Pecan Stuffed Peppers 43

29. Peas and Cashew Cream 44

30. Plaice and Peppers Pasta 45

31. Salmon and Tomato Rice 46

32. Zucchini Soup with Fenugreek Seeds and Spring Onion 47

33. Tilapia, Turmeric, and Almond Cream 48

34. Spicy Turnips and Shallot Soup 49

35. Zucchini Stuffed With Smoked Salmon and Soy Cheese 50

Main Course Dishes 52

4

36. Almond and Pepper Turkey 52

37. Avocado and Herbs Sauce Tilapia 54

38. Broccoli and Tuna Chipotle Stew 55

39. Cashew and Zucchini-Crusted Salmon 56

40. Cilantro Trout and Tomato 57

41. Coconut and Amchoor Chicken 59

42. Cumin, Honey, and Chia Seeds Chicken 60

43. Kale and Smoked Salmon Eggs 61

44. Tuna Brown Rice and Pecans Poke Bowl 62

45. Mint and Garam Masala Baked Halibut 63

46. Mushrooms and Cucumber Plaice 64

47. Peas and Zucchini Salmon 65

48. Pumpkin and Olives Turkey 66

49. Rosemary and Pine Nuts Crusted Turkey 67

50. Zucchini and Alaska Pollock Spicy Soup 68

Vegetarian Dishes 69

51. Broccoli and Cumin Tofu Croquettes 69

52. Kale and Soy Cheese Curry Cream 71

53. Peas, Lime, and Jalapeno Cream 72

54. Pepper, Cucumber, and Zucchini Salad 73

55. Tomatoes with Ginger-Vinegar Sauce 75

Gluten-Free Recipes 76

56. Chipotle, Chickpeas, and Spinach Mint Cream 76

57. Mango, Avocado, and Nuts Salad 78

58. Garlic and Zucchini Curry Tofu Soup 79

59. Tomato, Radicchio, and Hake Salad 80

60. Zucchini, Cucumber, and Egg Salad 81

Snack Recipes 82

61. Peaches in Orange, Cinnamon, and Coconut Syrup..82

62. Pineapple with Ginger-Pomegranate Cream 84

63. Oatmeal with Mango and Berries Cream 85

64. Pineapple, Plum, and Orange Juice 86

65. Vanilla and Pistachio Pudding 87

Smoothie Recipes 88

66. Apricot, Banana, and Ginger Smoothie 89

67. Avocado and Kiwi Smoothie 90

68. Mango and Melon Smoothie 91

Dessert Recipes 92

69. Cinnamon, Cumin, and Coconut Baked Apples 92

70. Peach, Ginger, and Orange Ice Cream 93

MEAL PLAN **94**

SHOPPING LIST **100**

Anti-Inflammatory Diet Guide

Inflammation is a natural physiological mechanism, which is necessary for our body to be able to heal and defend itself from damage caused by viruses and bacteria, which are the main cause of inflammation.

However, when inflammatory processes are repeated too often, inflammation becomes detrimental to health. In this case, we are talking about chronic inflammation. Chronic inflammation has a variable duration, it can last a few weeks but in the most serious cases, even years, causing harmful consequences for our bodies.

Having made this small premise, we can assure you that there are many things you can do to reduce inflammation and improve your general well-being.

Chapter 1: Inflammation and Anti-Inflammatory Diet

What Are the Causes of Inflammation?

Inflammation can be caused by microorganisms, chemicals, physical agents, tissue death, or inadequate immunological responses.

Among the most common stimuli are viruses and bacteria. Viruses destroy body cells, bacteria release endotoxins. Other possible causes are physical trauma, radiation, burns, frostbite, or contact with chemicals such as acids, oxidizing agents, or alkalis.

It can also be caused by a drop in blood flow to a specific area of the body.

Mini Guide on How to Behave and Avoid Risk Factors

In addition to infectious factors, i.e., caused by viruses or bacteria, lifestyle can also often favor the onset of inflammation. A practical example is given by the incorrect food style that we often follow lately due to lack of time to devote to healthy cooking. The consumption of high quantities of refined sugar or foods with a high fructose content can not only be harmful to health in general but also develop strong inflammatory states in our bodies. Furthermore, the main consequences of this incorrect lifestyle are insulin resistance, obesity, and finally, diabetes. Some research has in fact confirmed that the immoderate consumption of white bread, for example, has led to an increase in cases of insulin resistance and obesity in all parts of the world.

It has also been shown that frequent intake of processed and packaged foods, especially if they contain hydrogenated fats, not only causes inflammation but also damages the outer membrane (endothelium) that lines the arteries.

Another possible food guilty of increasing inflammatory levels are vegetable oils which are very often used in foods we buy ready-made at the supermarket. The constant consumption of these oils creates a shift in the balance between omega-3 and omega-6 that normally occurs in a healthy body.

It has also been shown that the regular consumption of alcoholic beverages, especially spirits, and fatty and overly processed meats trigger inflammation, especially in the liver.

The last risk factor is a sedentary lifestyle. The sedentary lifestyle, which involves spending entire days in front of the computer, is certainly not healthy in general, but it is also a major risk factor for inflammation.

The Importance of Diet to Fight Inflammation

If you are tired of constantly suffering from inflammatory states, the solution is simple, just abolish inflammatory foods from your diet and give space only to foods with anti-inflammatory power.

The perfect diet for those suffering from inflammation should be based on the consumption of whole foods rich in nutrients, with strong antioxidant power. On the other hand, processed foods with a high quantity of sugars or fatty oils of both vegetable and animal origin should be avoided.

Antioxidants, in particular, are indispensable if your goal is to reduce inflammation. This is because antioxidants manage to reduce the level of free radicals within our bodies. Free radicals are reactive molecules, which are naturally released in the body but can lead to inflammatory states when the production of these molecules goes out of control.

The perfect anti-inflammatory diet must have a healthy balance of macronutrients (protein, carbohydrates, and fat) and must be rich in vitamins, minerals, water, and fiber.

What Are the Foods to Avoid Drastically

There are certain categories of foods, which increase the risk of developing inflammatory states. For this reason, it would be necessary to completely abolish them from our diet, or, in any case, reduce them drastically. In particular, you should avoid:

- Sugary drinks and canned fruit juices as they contain high amounts of sugar and, in the case of sugary drinks, are totally devoid of nutrients.
- Refined carbohydrates, i.e., all those foods made with white flour such as pasta and bread.
- Sweets should be abolished due to their high sugar content and the imbalance that is generated between macro and micronutrients.
- Excessively processed meat, fatty cured meats, and sausages.
- Oil of vegetable origin that contain high contents of trans fats.
- Alcoholic beverages.

Foods That Should Not Be Missing in an Anti-Inflammatory Diet

To fight inflammation, the foods to include in the diet are:

- Vegetables, especially green leaves.
- Fruit, particularly fruit that has a dark and intense color, such as cherries or blueberries.
- Fruits with a high content of good fats such as olives or avocados.
- Fish with a high content of omega-3 and omega-6 fats such as cod, salmon, anchovies, mackerel, and sardines.
- Nuts and oilseeds.

- Legumes are an excellent source of vegetable protein but also an excellent source of fiber, folic acid, and an innumerable content of mineral salts and vitamins.

- Peppers and hot peppers.

- Dark chocolate with a high content of bitter cocoa.

- All kinds of spices.

- Egg.

- White and fat-free meats.

- Green tea.

- Extra virgin olive oil.

- Probiotics such as yogurt, kefir, kombucha, and kimchi.

However, keep in mind that no single food will boost a person's health or protect them from inflammation. It is therefore important to include a large variety of nutritious and healthy foods in our daily diet and, above all, to pay attention to various and alternate protein sources.

Inflammation, Intolerances, and Allergies

It has been shown that some substances and some foods, which contain allergens, can trigger the inflammatory response in our bodies. In particular:

- **Foods containing gluten:** Many people have strong inflammatory reactions whenever they consume foods containing gluten. Gluten-free diets are very restrictive and therefore cannot be followed easily or for long periods of time. The anti-inflammatory diet could be the ideal solution, as it reduces the intake of gluten by replacing it with healthier foods and is not very restrictive. It can also be followed for a long time and with much more ease.

- **Nightshade:** Plants belonging to the nightshade family seem to trigger flare-ups in those suffering from inflammatory diseases. However, there is no certain evidence that these foods trigger inflammation. In fact, clinical studies have also shown the disconnect between belladonna plants and inflammation, as some plants belonging to this category, such as tomatoes and peppers are known for their anti-inflammatory properties. The nightshade problem arises when you are intolerant or allergic to these plants or to some key elements of their composition, such as nickel, for example. In these cases, it is better to consult an allergist and find out if the cause of the inflammation is not really an allergic reaction.

Chapter 2: The Best Anti-Inflammatory Supplements

Food supplements are products intended to supplement the normal diet when the right number of vitamins or mineral salts is not taken.

Many components can make up food supplements, ranging from vitamins to minerals, fatty acids, and herbs.

What is important to underline is that food supplements are not intended as a substitute for a varied and balanced healthy diet and a healthy lifestyle.

Moving on to the inflammatory part, the best supplements are:

Curcumin

Curcumin is a substance found in high concentrations of turmeric; a spice widely used in Indian cuisine. It is well-known thanks to its typical bright yellow color. Curcumin appears to be useful in reducing inflammatory states in diseases such as diabetes, inflammatory bowel disease, rheumatoid arthritis, and osteoarthritis. However, curcumin is not absorbed in our body since we take very little amount with food.

If you want to boost curcumin to have its powerful health benefits, you can take it in supplement form. However, remember that over 500 mg of curcumin per day can lead to side symptoms such as headache or nausea and intestinal problems.

Ginger

Ginger, in addition to being a spice widely used in cooking, is used as a home remedy to treat symptoms such as nausea or indigestion. It has been found that two of the main components of ginger, gingerol and zingerone, are useful for reducing inflammation. Ginger-based supplements can therefore help you solve the inflammation problem. However, never exceed the daily dose of 2 g per day, as ginger in large doses can have a blood-thinning effect. Furthermore, the use of extra doses of ginger is not recommended if you are taking anticoagulant drugs.

Spirulina

Spirulina is an alga with known antioxidant effects. Spirulina intake, therefore, helps to reduce inflammation. It also strengthens the immune system and improves life expectancy. Spirulina supplements are basically powders that must be added to the preparations in the kitchen or in smoothies or juices. Remember not to take more than 8 g of spirulina per day. Furthermore, although no significant side effects have been found, people suffering from autoimmune diseases should avoid taking supplements based on this seaweed.

Vitamin D

Vitamin D is an essential element for the well-being of the body, as it increases the immune system and has a strong anti-inflammatory effect. In fact, many studies have found a close correlation between vitamin D deficiency and inflammatory processes. Supplementing with vitamin D, especially if you have a deficiency, is essential for the anti-inflammatory response. However, periodically check the levels of vitamin D in the blood, because too high levels of this vitamin can be toxic to the body.

Bromelain

Bromelain is an enzyme found in large quantities in pineapples. Bromelain has excellent anti-inflammatory power, comparable to that of NSAIDs (non-steroidal anti-inflammatory drugs), but without the typical side effects of drugs. Bromelain-based supplements contain an amount of this substance equal to 500 mg. These supplements are quite safe and no major side effects are reported in their use.

Chapter 3: Recipes

Breakfast Recipes

1. Apricot, Pistachio, and Cinnamon Yogurt Bowl

PREPARATION TIME: 10 minutes

DIFFICULTY LEVEL: Easy

CALORIES: 160

NUTRITIONAL VALUES: CARBS: 22 G; PROTEIN: 5 G; FAT: 9 G

INGREDIENTS FOR 2 SERVINGS

- 1 cup of low-fat white yogurt
- 2 pinches of cinnamon
- 4 apricots
- 2 tsp honey
- 2 tsp chopped pistachios

DIRECTIONS

1. Start this very simple recipe by peeling, pitting, and washing the 4 apricots, then slicing.
2. Put the plain low-fat yogurt in two bowls and season each with a pinch of cinnamon and 1 tsp honey.
3. Place the chopped apricots on top of the yogurt.
4. Sprinkle with chopped pistachios and serve.

2. Avocado, Vanilla, and Chocolate Toast

PREPARATION TIME: 15 minutes

COOKING TIME: 5 minutes

CALORIES: 370

NUTRITIONAL VALUES: CARBS: 48 G; PROTEIN: 7 G; FAT: 14 G

INGREDIENTS FOR 2 SERVINGS

- 2 slices of wholemeal bread
- ½ avocado
- 1 tbsp chopped dark chocolate
- 2 tsp honey
- 1 tsp vanilla extract

DIRECTIONS

1. Start this breakfast recipe by peeling the avocado. Take half pulp, pit, and split the half avocado into some small pieces. Then, arrange these avocado pieces in a bowl.
2. Mash the avocado with a fork and then add the honey and vanilla extract. Start to mix.
3. Arrange the slices of bread in the toaster and toast them until they are quite crispy and brown outside.
4. Arrange the just toasted bread in two serving dishes and spread the avocado vanilla and honey cream on the surface.
5. Sprinkle with the chopped chocolate on top and serve.

3. Banana and Kiwi Milkshake

PREPARATION TIME: 15 minutes

CALORIES: 130

NUTRITIONAL VALUES: CARBS: 38 G; PROTEIN: 2 G; FAT: 4 G

INGREDIENTS FOR 2 SERVINGS

- 1 ripe banana
- 3 kiwis
- ½ cup sugar-free soy milk
- ½ tsp ground cinnamon
- 4 ice cubes

DIRECTIONS

1. The first step for this recipe is to peel the banana and kiwis and split both into little slices.
2. Put the banana and kiwi slices in the glass of the blender and blend for 30–40 seconds.
3. Now add the cinnamon and soy milk and blend for another minute.
4. Then add the 4 ice cubes and turn on the blender until you have a thick and homogeneous milkshake.
5. Transfer the banana and kiwi cinnamon milkshake into the glasses, add the straws, and serve.

4. Cabbage and Jalapeno Frittata

PREPARATION TIME: 10 minutes

COOKING TIME: 10 minutes

CALORIES: 180

NUTRITIONAL VALUES: CARBS: 2 G; PROTEIN: 13 G; FAT: 7 G

INGREDIENTS FOR 2 SERVINGS

- 2 eggs
- ½ cup sugar-free almond milk
- 2 oz chopped cabbage leaves
- 1 chopped jalapeno
- Salt and pepper to taste
- Olive oil to taste

DIRECTIONS

1. The first step in this recipe is to crack the 2 eggs into a bowl. Now add the almond milk together with the jalapeño, salt, and pepper. Beat the eggs with the help of a fork.
2. Pour now a little olive oil into a non-stick pan.
3. Place half of the jalapeno mixture into the pan, let it cook for 3 minutes, and then turn it over.
4. Put half of the just minced kale leaves inside, close the omelet in two, and cook for another 2–3 minutes.
5. Repeat the same operation with the other half of the mixture.
6. Once the cabbage and jalapeno frittatas are ready, transfer them to two serving plates, and serve.

5. Cucumber and Strawberry Toast

PREPARATION TIME: 15 minutes

COOKING TIME: 10 minutes

CALORIES: 260

NUTRITIONAL VALUES: CARBS: 25 G; PROTEIN: 10 G; FAT: 4 G

INGREDIENTS FOR 2 SERVINGS

- 4 very little slices of wholemeal bread
- ½ cucumber
- 2 eggs
- 2 oz sliced strawberries
- 2 tsp honey
- 1 tsp cumin powder
- 1 tsp vanilla extract
- 1 cup sugar-free oat milk
- Olive oil to taste
- Salt to taste

DIRECTIONS

1. Begin by cracking the 2 eggs into a bowl. Then add the eggs, salt, oat milk, and cumin powder.
2. Beat the mixture with the help of a manual whisk until you get a homogeneous mixture.
3. Add 2 slices of bread to the mixture and turn them over.
4. Grease a non-stick frying pan with a little oil and cook the slices of bread for 2–3 minutes.
5. Now do the same operation with the other two slices of bread.
6. It's time to prepare the cucumber. Peel it and cut it into cubes.
7. Put the cucumber cubes in a non-stick pan and sauté them with the honey and vanilla extract. Cook it for about 5 minutes.
8. Once the vanilla cucumber is ready, turn it off and put the slices of bread on the serving dishes. Then add the sliced cucumber and strawberries and serve up this delicious anti-inflammatory breakfast.

6. Ginger and Avocado Pancakes

PREPARATION TIME: 15 minutes

COOKING TIME: 15 minutes

DIFFICULTY LEVEL: Easy

CALORIES: 270

NUTRITIONAL VALUES: CARBS: 16 G; PROTEIN: 6 G; FAT: 20 G

INGREDIENTS FOR 2 SERVINGS

- 1 ripe avocado
- ¼ cup coconut flour
- 1 tbsp oat flour
- 1 tsp ginger powder
- 2 eggs
- 1 tsp honey
- 1 pinch of baking powder
- Olive oil to taste

DIRECTIONS

1. Start this anti-inflammatory pancake by peeling and pitting the ripe avocado, then cut it into small pieces and transfer it to a bowl.
2. Mash it with a fork. Do it until you get a smooth and creamy mixture.
3. Crack the two eggs into the bowl with the avocado puree, then beat with an electric mixer until smooth.
4. Add the ginger powder, honey, oat, and coconut flour now and start mixing with a wooden spoon.
5. Once well incorporated, add the baking powder.
6. Stir again, adding 1 tbsp olive oil.
7. Next, grease a nonstick skillet with very little oil and spoon some of the ginger-avocado mixture into the center.

8. Once the mixture starts to have some bubbles on its surface, turn it over and continue cooking for another 2–3 minutes.

9. Repeat the same steps for all the pancakes.

10. Once ready, divide the avocado and ginger pancakes into two serving dishes and serve.

7. Mango, Almonds, and Egg Toast

PREPARATION TIME: 15 minutes

COOKING TIME: 5 minutes

CALORIES: 270

NUTRITIONAL VALUES: CARBS: 29 G; PROTEIN: 10 G; FAT: 9 G

INGREDIENTS FOR 2 SERVINGS

- 2 slices of wholemeal bread
- 1 ripe mango
- 1 tsp turmeric powder
- 2 tsp almond flakes
- 2 hard-boiled eggs
- Olive oil to taste
- Salt and pepper to taste

DIRECTIONS

1. Start this breakfast recipe by boiling the eggs for 8–9 minutes in a boiling water pot. Once cooked, let cool, peel, and halve the 2 eggs.

2. Meanwhile, arrange the slices of bread in a toaster, and toast them until crispy and golden on the outside.

3. Once toasted, transfer the slices of bread to two serving plates, add a little olive oil, and season with salt and pepper.

4. Peel the mango, cut it in half, pit it, and remove the pulp.

5. Place the mango pulp in a bowl, mash it with the help of a fork, and then season it with oil, turmeric powder, salt, and pepper.

6. Spread the turmeric mango pulp on the slices of bread, put the halved boiled eggs on top, sprinkle with almond flakes, and serve.

8. Peanuts, Coconut, and Ginger Muffins

PREPARATION TIME: 15 minutes

COOKING TIME: 20 minutes

CALORIES: 310

NUTRITIONAL VALUES: CARBS: 29 G; PROTEIN: 12 G; FAT: 12 G

INGREDIENTS FOR 2 SERVINGS

- ⅓ cup coconut flour
- 1 tbsp chopped peanuts
- 2 tbsp coconut milk
- 1 tsp ginger powder
- 1 egg
- 1 tbsp raw honey
- 1 pinch of salt
- ¼ cup olive oil
- ½ tsp baking powder
- The grated zest of ½ orange

DIRECTIONS

1. Place the ¼ cup of olive oil and the honey in a bowl and, using an electric mixer, beat the ingredients until smooth.
2. Add the egg and continue beating until the egg is fully incorporated.
3. Add salt, orange zest, and ginger powder, and continue beating.
4. Now, add the 2 tbsp of coconut milk and whisk again.
5. At this point, add the baking powder, coconut flour, and peanuts and mix with the help of a spatula until you get a smooth mixture.
6. Take 4 cupcake liners and place 4 paper cups inside.
7. Pour the coconut and peanut mixture into the cups and cook in the oven at 375°F for about 20 minutes.
8. After 20 minutes, check the cooking with a toothpick and if they are still not ready, continue cooking for another 5 minutes.
9. Once cooked, take the anti-inflammatory muffins out of the oven, let them cool, and serve.

9. Spicy Pecan Cookies

PREPARATION TIME: 15 minutes

COOKING TIME: 12 minutes

CALORIES: 80

NUTRITIONAL VALUES: CARBS: 8 G; PROTEIN: 3 G; FAT: 7 G

INGREDIENTS FOR 2 SERVINGS

- 2 tbsp wholemeal flour
- 2 tbsp finely chopped pecans
- 1 tsp ginger powder
- 1 egg
- 1 pinch of nutmeg
- 1 tbsp honey
- 1 tbsp olive oil
- ½ lemon

DIRECTIONS

1. Start this spicy cookie recipe by putting the wholemeal flour, chopped pecans, nutmeg, ginger powder, olive oil, and honey in the blender jar.
2. Once this is done, turn on the blender and blend until a very homogeneous mixture is created.
3. Then, pour the newly obtained mixture onto a pastry board and add the zest of half a lemon and, finally, the beaten egg.
4. Start working this mixture quickly enough, helping yourself with your fingers.
5. The dough should be quite homogeneous and without lumps.
6. Cover the freshly prepared dough with transparent film and let it rest for an hour in the fridge.
7. After this time, add a little whole wheat flour to a work surface, and roll out the rested cookie dough with a rolling pin.
8. Next, cut the dough into the shape of the cookies that you desire.
9. Take a skillet and line it with parchment paper.
10. Place the spicy cookies inside and cook them at 338°F for 10–12 minutes.
11. Once cooked, take the pecans spicy cookies out of the oven and let them cool before serving.

10. Turkey and Cumin Scrambled Egg Toast

PREPARATION TIME: 10 minutes

DIFFICULTY LEVEL: Easy

CALORIES: 330

NUTRITIONAL VALUES: CARBS: 22 G; PROTEIN: 25 G; FAT: 7 G

INGREDIENTS FOR 2 SERVINGS

- 2 slices of wholemeal bread of 1.7 oz each
- 1.7 oz roasted turkey slices
- 2 eggs
- 1 tsp cumin powder
- 1 tsp chili powder
- Salt to taste
- Olive oil to taste

DIRECTIONS

1. Start by arranging the slices of bread in a toaster, and toast them until they are quite crispy on the outside.
2. Once toasted, place the slices of bread on 2 serving plates, brush them with some olive oil, and season with chili powder.
3. Pour a little olive oil into a non-stick pan and, once hot, crack the two eggs inside.
4. Stir with a wooden spoon, cook for 5 minutes, then season with salt and cumin powder and turn off the heat.
5. Spread the turkey slices on the bread and put the cumin scrambled eggs on top.
6. You can now serve this anti-inflammatory breakfast.

Appetizers

11. Beetroot and Ginger Eggs

PREPARATION TIME: 20 minutes

COOKING TIME: 10 minutes

CALORIES: 140

NUTRITIONAL VALUES: CARBS: 2 G; PROTEIN: 15 G; FAT: 8 G

INGREDIENTS FOR 2 SERVINGS

- 2 large size eggs
- 1 cooked beetroot
- 1 tsp ginger powder
- ½ cup cold water
- 1 tbsp apple cider vinegar
- Salt and pepper to taste

DIRECTIONS

1. As a first step, put the 2 eggs in a saucepan and cover them completely with cold water.

2. Bring to a boil and then keep on cooking the eggs for another 8 minutes.

3. After the cooking time, rinse the eggs under cold water and peel them.

4. Now, cut the beets into cubes and arrange them in a bowl.

5. Add the apple cider vinegar, cold water, ginger powder, salt, and pepper.

6. Take an immersion blender and blend everything until you will have a homogeneous and liquid mixture.

7. Now put the eggs into the bowl and coat them with the beetroot juice.

8. Place cling film over the bowl and transfer to the fridge to marinate for 2 hours.

9. After 2 hours, remove the eggs from the fridge.

10. Dry them with a paper towel, cut them in half, put them on a plate, and serve them as an appetizer.

12. Carrot and Soy Cheese-Filled Lettuce

PREPARATION TIME: 20 minutes

COOKING TIME: 8 minutes

CALORIES: 180

NUTRITIONAL VALUES: CARBS: 10 G; PROTEIN: 20 G; FAT: 6 G

INGREDIENTS FOR 2 SERVINGS

- 4 large romaine lettuce leaves
- 3.5 oz cubed carrot
- 4 tbsp soy cheese
- 2 tsp honey
- 2 tsp apple cider vinegar
- Salt and pepper to taste
- Chia seeds

DIRECTIONS

1. The first step for this recipe is to wash the 4 lettuce leaves and dry them.
2. Now, put the soy cheese in a bowl.
3. Add the honey, carrot, and apple cider vinegar and mix everything together.
4. Add a pinch of salt and pepper and mix all the ingredients.
5. Take the whole lettuce leaves and fill them with the cheese and carrot mixture. Arrange them in such a way that they look like a bowl.
6. Finish decorating the lettuce leaves with chia seeds and serve.

13. Soy Cheese and Papaya Dish

PREPARATION TIME: 10 minutes

COOKING TIME: 15 minutes

CALORIES: 260

NUTRITIONAL VALUES: CARBS: 10 G; PROTEIN: 16 G; FAT: 12 G

INGREDIENTS FOR 4 SERVINGS

- 7 oz cubed soy cheese
- ½ scallion
- 1 cubed papaya
- ½ tsp chopped rosemary
- Olive oil to taste
- Salt and pepper to taste

DIRECTIONS

1. First, clean and remove the filaments and seeds from the papaya, then wash and cut its pulp into cubes.
2. Peel and wash the scallion too and cut it into thin slices.
3. Brush a baking pan with some olive oil.
4. Place the cubed soy cheese in the center of it.
5. Now add the scallion slices and papaya cubes.
6. Season everything with oil, chopped rosemary, salt, and pepper, and bake at 392°F for 15 minutes.
7. Once ready, take this anti-inflammatory appetizer from the oven and serve.

14. Orange and Chili Avocado

PREPARATION TIME: 15 minutes

DIFFICULTY LEVEL: Easy

CALORIES: 190

NUTRITIONAL VALUES: CARBS: 3 G; PROTEIN: 5 G; FAT: 18 G

INGREDIENTS FOR 2 SERVINGS

- 1 avocado
- 1 tsp chia seeds (divided)
- 1 tsp chili powder
- Juice of 1 orange
- 2 tsp olive oil
- Salt and pepper to taste

DIRECTIONS

1. As the first step for this very easy snack recipe, peel the avocado, pit it, and cut the pulp into slices.
2. Now, arrange the avocado slices in a serving dish and season it with orange juice, chili powder, oil, salt, and pepper.
3. Sprinkle with the chia seeds and serve.

15. Papaya and Cherry Fruit Salad

PREPARATION TIME: 15 minutes

CALORIES: 200

NUTRITIONAL VALUES: CARBS: 34 G; PROTEIN: 2 G; FAT: 3 G

INGREDIENTS FOR 2 SERVINGS

- 10 pitted cherries
- 1 papaya
- 2 tsp coconut flour
- 3 tbsp sugar-free coconut milk
- 1 tsp honey

DIRECTIONS

1. Start by peeling the papaya with a sharp knife, split the fruit in half, and, by using a spoon, remove the seeds along with the filaments. Then cut the fruit into cubes.
2. Once this is done, cut the cherries in half.
3. Put the cherries and papaya in a bowl.
4. Now, in a small bowl, combine the coconut milk and honey, and then cover the papaya and cherries with this mixture.
5. Stir gently and then transfer to the fridge for at least 30 minutes.
6. After 30 minutes, spoon the fruit salad into 2 bowls, sprinkle with coconut flour, and serve.

16. Peas, Avocado, and Garlic Cream

PREPARATION TIME: 10 minutes

COOKING TIME: 20 minutes

CALORIES: 390

NUTRITIONAL VALUES: CARBS: 24 G; PROTEIN: 15 G; FAT: 22 G

INGREDIENTS FOR 2 SERVINGS

- 7 oz fresh peas
- 1 ripe avocado
- 2 cups vegetable broth
- 2 bay leaves
- 1 garlic clove
- Salt and pepper to taste
- Olive oil to taste

DIRECTIONS

1. Start by rinsing the peas under running water and then let them drain.
2. Peel the garlic and brown it in a pan with olive oil and bay leaves.
3. Add the drained peas, salt, and pepper; mix, and cook for a few seconds. Then add the vegetable broth.
4. Cook for 20 minutes, stirring occasionally.
5. Once the peas are cooked, take an immersion blender and blend together with the pitted and diced avocado until you get a fairly smooth cream.
6. Pour the pea and avocado cream onto 2 serving plates and serve as an appetizer.

17. Soy Cheese and Fruit Bowl

PREPARATION TIME: 20 minutes

DIFFICULTY LEVEL: Easy

CALORIES: 230

NUTRITIONAL VALUES: CARBS: 28 G; PROTEIN: 10 G; FAT: 3 G

INGREDIENTS FOR 2 SERVINGS

- 7 oz soy cheese
- 2 apples
- 4 cherries
- 10 raspberries
- 1 tsp vanilla extract
- 1 tsp ground cinnamon
- 1 tbsp honey

DIRECTIONS

1. As the first step for this recipe, place the soy cheese, vanilla, cinnamon, and honey in a bowl. Stir with the help of a fork until you get a soft and homogeneous cream.
2. Wash and pit the cherries and cut them into pieces.
3. Peel the apples, remove the seeds, and cut them into slices.
4. Wash and dry the raspberries too.
5. Put the vanilla and cinnamon soy cheese cream in the bottom of 2 little bowls.
6. Add the cut fruit on top and serve this snack recipe.

18. Pumpkin, Almond, and Cumin Flan

PREPARATION TIME: 30 minutes

COOKING TIME: 25 minutes

CALORIES: 230

NUTRITIONAL VALUES: CARBS: 12 G; PROTEIN: 8 G; FAT: 7 G

INGREDIENTS FOR 2 SERVINGS

- 17 oz squash pulp
- 2 eggs
- 1 cup sugar-free almond milk
- 1 tsp chopped dill
- 1 tsp cumin powder
- Olive oil to taste
- Salt and pepper to taste

DIRECTIONS

1. As a first step, wash and dry the pumpkin pulp.
2. Cut the pumpkin pulp into cubes and steam for 20 minutes.
3. Once the time has elapsed, drain the pumpkin and let it cool.
4. Transfer the squash to a bowl.
5. Add salt, pepper, dill, cumin powder, almond milk, and eggs to the bowl.
6. Blend everything with an immersion blender.
7. Grease a round frying pan with olive oil and pour the pumpkin and cumin mixture inside.

8. Bake at 338°F for 25 minutes.

9. Once the flan is cooked, take it out of the oven and let it cool.

10. Cut the pumpkin flan into slices and serve.

19. Tuna and Honey-Stuffed Pumpkin

PREPARATION TIME: 15 minutes

COOKING TIME: 5 minutes

CALORIES: 300

NUTRITIONAL VALUES: CARBS: 14 G; PROTEIN: 26 G; FAT: 13 G

INGREDIENTS FOR 2 SERVINGS

- 4 pumpkin slices
- 3.5 oz drained canned tuna
- 2 tbsp honey
- 1 tsp turmeric powder
- 1 tsp chopped mint
- Olive oil to taste
- Salt and pepper to taste.

DIRECTIONS

1. Start the recipe by draining the canned tuna.

2. Then, arrange the tuna in a bowl, add the turmeric powder, honey, salt, pepper, and a little olive oil, and mix everything together.

3. Fill each pumpkin slice with the tuna mixture, garnish with chopped mint, and serve as an appetizer.

20. Zucchini and Tomato Sandwich

PREPARATION TIME: 15 minutes

COOKING TIME: 2 minutes

CALORIES: 320

NUTRITIONAL VALUES: CARBS: 38 G; PROTEIN: 5 G; FAT: 3 G

INGREDIENTS FOR 2 SERVINGS

- 4 slices of whole meal sandwich bread
- 8 slices of zucchini
- 2 tbsp chopped tomatoes
- 1 tsp chopped chives

DIRECTIONS

1. The first thing to do is arrange the slices of bread in the toaster and let them brown for a couple of minutes.
2. Once ready, transfer the slices of bread to a cutting board.
3. Put the chopped tomatoes, zucchini slices, and finally the chives on 2 slices of bread.
4. Close with the other slices of bread and serve as an appetizer.

First-Course Dishes

21. Pasta with Chicken, Asparagus, and Leeks

PREPARATION TIME: 20 minutes

COOKING TIME: 25 minutes

CALORIES: 450

NUTRITIONAL VALUES: CARBS: 42 G; PROTEIN: 29 G; FAT: 14 G

INGREDIENTS FOR 2 SERVINGS

- 3.5 oz wholemeal penne pasta
- 7 oz cleaned chicken breast
- 2.5 oz asparagus
- 2 leeks
- 1 tbsp chopped spring onion
- Zest of ½ lemon
- Olive oil to taste
- Salt and pepper to taste

DIRECTIONS

1. Wash and dry the chicken breast, after having removed all the fat excess, and then cut it into strips.

2. Trim now all the asparagus, rinse, and then cut them into pieces. Do the same with spring onions and leeks. Boil the three veggies in boiling water and salt for 10 minutes.

3. After 10 minutes, drain and set aside.

4. Heat a spoonful of olive oil in a pan and put the veggies to brown.

5. Once they are golden, add the chicken strips.

6. Season with salt and pepper and cook for 15 minutes.

7. Meanwhile, place a pot of water and salt to a boil and then add the penne pasta to cook, following the cooking times indicated on the package (or cook for about 12 minutes).

8. Once cooked, drain the pasta and transfer it to the pan with the asparagus, leeks, and chicken.

9. Stir, combine well, and then put the chicken asparagus pasta into serving dishes.

10. Sprinkle with some lemon zest and serve.

22. Avocado and Turkey Cream

PREPARATION TIME: 15 minutes

COOKING TIME: 30 minutes

CALORIES: 290

NUTRITIONAL VALUES: CARBS: 10 G; PROTEIN: 6 G; FAT: 22 G

INGREDIENTS FOR 2 SERVINGS

- 1 ripe avocado
- 1 tbsp chopped onion
- 3.5 oz minced turkey breast, cleaned
- 1 pink grapefruit
- ½ cup low-fat white yogurt
- 3 cups vegetable broth
- 1 tsp chopped cilantro leaves
- Salt and pepper to taste
- Olive oil to taste

DIRECTIONS

1. Start this anti-inflammatory first-course recipe by peeling the avocado; remove the seed, remove the pulp, and cut it into cubes.
2. Wash and dry the pink grapefruit too and grate its zest.
3. Wash and dry the cilantro leaves, then chop too.
4. Then, pour 2 tsp of olive oil into a pan and let it heat.
5. Once hot, put the onion to brown for 2 minutes.
6. Now, add the avocado and minced turkey; mix and sauté for 2–3 minutes, stirring often.
7. Add the vegetable stock and chopped cilantro leaves, cover with a lid, and cook for about 10 minutes.
8. After the cooking time has passed, season with a pinch of salt and pepper.
9. Then, place all the content in a bowl.
10. Now, you should take an immersion blender, add the grapefruit zest, and blend until you get a thick and very homogeneous cream.
11. Finally, add the low-fat yogurt and stir everything well.
12. Place the avocado and turkey cream on serving plates and serve.

23. Chipotle Chicken and Bean Soup

PREPARATION TIME: 20 minutes

COOKING TIME: 1 hour and 30 minutes

CALORIES: 290

NUTRITIONAL VALUES: CARBS: 34 G; PROTEIN: 15 G; FAT: 3 G

INGREDIENTS FOR 2 SERVINGS

- 7 oz chicken breast, already cleaned
- 7 oz broad beans, already boiled
- 1 tsp chopped chipotle
- 1 scallion
- ½ cup apple cider vinegar
- 1 tbsp chopped parsley leaves
- Olive oil to taste
- Salt and pepper to taste

DIRECTIONS

1. Start the recipe by rinsing the already cleaned chicken breast (skinless and fatless) under running water; let it drain and cut it into cubes.
2. Now, peel and wash the scallion and then chop it.
3. Heat some olive oil in a saucepan and arrange the scallion and chopped chipotle to brown for 1 minute.
4. After this operation, add the chicken cubes.
5. Cook the chicken for 4–5 minutes.
6. Now add 1 cup of hot water and apple cider vinegar and cook for another 5 minutes.
7. Let it evaporate and add the broad beans.
8. Cook for another 5 minutes and add a pinch of salt and pepper.
9. After the cooking time has passed, turn off and let the chicken and broad beans rest for 2 minutes.
10. Now put the broad beans and chicken soup on the plates, season it with a bit of olive oil, sprinkle with chopped parsley, and serve.

24. Cabbage and Scallop Rice

PREPARATION TIME: 10 minutes

COOKING TIME: 40 minutes

CALORIES: 410

NUTRITIONAL VALUES: CARBS: 48 G; PROTEIN: 13 G; FAT: 4 G

INGREDIENTS FOR 2 SERVINGS

- 3.5 oz brown rice
- 2 tbsp olive oil
- 7 oz already cooked scallops
- 7 oz already boiled cabbage leaves
- 4 cups vegetable broth
- Salt and pepper to taste

DIRECTIONS

1. Arrange the boiled cabbage leaves in the blender jar and blend until smooth.
2. Now heat some olive oil in a saucepan and pour the brown rice to toast for a couple of minutes.
3. Add 3 cups of vegetable stock and stir the brown rice constantly.
4. Once the stock is completely absorbed, add another ladle and keep on mixing.
5. You should do this operation until the rice is totally cooked.
6. Once the rice is ready, add the cabbage purée and cooked scallops and mix well.
7. Add salt and pepper, stir again, and then turn off.
8. Now put the scallops and cabbage brown rice on 2 plates and serve.

25. Chickpea, Tuna, and Dill Soup

PREPARATION TIME: 15 minutes

COOKING TIME: 35 minutes

CALORIES: 390

NUTRITIONAL VALUES: CARBS: 20 G; PROTEIN: 21 G; FAT: 13 G

INGREDIENTS FOR 2 SERVINGS

- 10.5 oz tuna fillet
- 3.5 oz already boiled chickpeas
- 1 small size carrot
- 2 cups vegetable stock
- 1 red onion
- 1 tsp chopped dill
- Salt and pepper to taste
- Olive oil to taste

DIRECTIONS

1. First, heat up the vegetable stock.
2. Meanwhile, wash and dry the dill leaves and chop.
3. Peel both the carrot and red onion, wash them and chop them finely too.
4. Rinse the boiled chickpeas under running water and then leave them to drain.
5. Wash and dry the tuna fillet and then cube it.
6. Heat a little olive oil in a saucepan and then brown the pieces of carrot and onion, then add the chopped dill.
7. Cook for 2 minutes, add the tuna cubes, and sauté for 5 minutes.
8. Now add the chickpeas and mix.
9. Sauté for 5 minutes and coat everything with the hot vegetable broth.
10. Boil and then season with salt and pepper and keep cooking for 10 minutes.
11. After this time, remove the tuna fillet and keep it aside.
12. Continue cooking the chickpeas for another 10 minutes.
13. Once the time has elapsed, turn off and remove the dill leaves.
14. Put the chickpeas and the broth on serving plates.
15. Add the tuna cubes and serve.

26. Cod, Pine Nuts, and Quinoa Curry

PREPARATION TIME: 20 minutes

COOKING TIME: 15 minutes

CALORIES: 320

NUTRITIONAL VALUES: CARBS: 28 G; PROTEIN: 9 G; FAT: 10 G

INGREDIENTS FOR 2 SERVINGS

- 3.5 oz quinoa
- 3.5 oz already cubed and boiled cod
- 3 cups vegetable broth
- 2 tbsp chopped pine nuts
- 1 tsp curry powder
- A pinch of ground cinnamon
- 1 tsp chopped basil leaves
- Olive oil to taste
- Salt and pepper to taste

DIRECTIONS

1. The first step for this recipe is to rinse quickly the quinoa under running water and leave to drain it.
2. Pour the broth directly into a saucepan and bring it to a boil.
3. Once boiling, add the curry powder and the quinoa and let boil for about 15 minutes.
4. Once this cooking time has passed, let the quinoa rest in the cooking water for at least 3 minutes.
5. Drain the quinoa and let it cool.
6. Cut now the boiled cod into some cubes.
7. Toast and chop 2 tbsp of pine nuts and transfer it to a bowl with the cod cubes.
8. Now add the drained quinoa, chopped basil leaves, and cinnamon and mix.
9. Season with a bit of oil, salt, and pepper; stir and serve this first-course recipe.

27. Spicy Kale Cream

PREPARATION TIME: 10 minutes

COOKING TIME: 15 minutes

CALORIES: 85

NUTRITIONAL VALUES: CARBS: 3 G; PROTEIN: 8 G; FAT: 2 G

INGREDIENTS FOR 2 SERVINGS

- ½ kale
- 1 tsp ginger powder
- 2 tsp turmeric powder
- 1 tsp cumin powder
- ½ scallion
- 1 tbsp extra virgin olive oil + a drizzle to season
- Juice of 1 orange
- Salt and pepper
- ¼ cup water
- 1 tsp chopped mint leaves

DIRECTIONS

1. Start by washing and splitting the kale into leaves, removing the final part.
2. Season the kale leaves with a drizzle of extra virgin olive oil and a pinch of salt.
3. Let them cook in a preheated oven at 338°F for 15 minutes, or until they will be softened enough.

4. In the meantime, peel and chop the scallion.

5. Once it has softened, remove the kale from the oven and allow it to cool.

6. Place the kale into the food processor together with the turmeric, ginger, cumin, orange juice, olive oil, scallion, a pinch of pepper, and ¼ cup of water.

7. Blend all the ingredients well until you get a smooth cream.

8. You can now serve your spicy kale cream with a sprinkle of chopped mint on top.

28. Rice and Pecan Stuffed Peppers

PREPARATION TIME: 20 minutes

COOKING TIME: 15 minutes

CALORIES: 370

NUTRITIONAL VALUES: CARBS: 40 G; PROTEIN: 11 G; FAT: 3 G

INGREDIENTS

- 3.5 oz of already-cooked brown rice
- 2 large size yellow pepper
- 2.5 oz cubed carrot
- 2 tsp chopped pecans
- 2 sage leaves
- 1 tsp onion powder
- Zest of ½ lime
- Salt and pepper to taste
- Olive oil to taste

DIRECTIONS

1. The first step for this recipe is to take the just-cooked brown rice and leave it to cool.
2. Now, wash, remove the seeds and filaments, and empty the peppers.
3. Season with salt and oil and cook the peppers at 392°F for about 15 minutes. Then remove the peppers from the oven and let them chill.
4. Next, peel and wash the carrot and then cut it into cubes.
5. Wash the sage leaves and chop them.
6. Take the bowl with the brown rice back and add the diced carrot, chopped sage, walnuts, and lime zest.
7. Season with oil, onion powder, salt, and pepper and stir all these ingredients well.
8. Stuff the yellow bell peppers with the carrot-walnut-brown rice-sage mixture, transfer to 2 plates, and serve.

29. Peas and Cashew Cream

PREPARATION TIME: 10 minutes

COOKING TIME: 15 minutes

CALORIES: 160

NUTRITIONAL VALUES: CARBS: 16 G; PROTEIN: 9 G; FAT: 2 GR

INGREDIENTS FOR 2 SERVINGS

- 7 oz fresh peas
- 2 tbsp chopped cashews
- 1 tsp garam masala powder
- 2 tsp olive oil
- Juice of ½ lime
- 2 tsp chopped dill
- ¼ scallion
- Salt and pepper to taste

DIRECTIONS

1. First, boil the peas for 10 minutes in a little boiling water and let them drain.
2. Chop the cashews very finely.
3. Peel and chop the scallion too.
4. Pour the freshly chopped cashews into the food processor together with the drained peas, garam masala, dill, olive oil, scallion, and lime juice, and season with salt and pepper.
5. Next, turn on your food processor and puree everything until you get a smooth and creamy mixture.
6. Once soft, serve this delicious peas and cashews cream.

30. Plaice and Peppers Pasta

PREPARATION TIME: 20 minutes

COOKING TIME: 15 minutes

CALORIES: 420

NUTRITIONAL VALUES: CARBS: 51 G; PROTEIN: 18 G; FAT: 6 G

INGREDIENTS FOR 2 SERVINGS

- 3.5 oz whole-meal pasta
- 7 oz plaice fillet
- 1 small green pepper
- 1 tsp curry powder
- ½ onion
- 1 tsp cardamom seeds
- 1 cup water
- 1 tsp chopped chives
- Salt and pepper to taste
- Olive oil to taste

DIRECTIONS

1. Start by bringing the water to a boil and then cook the pasta for 10–12 minutes.
2. In the meantime, wash the plaice, remove the bones, pat it dry with paper towels, and then divide it into cubes.
3. Remove the cap, the seeds, and the white filaments from the green pepper, and then wash it and split it into cubes as well.
4. Peel the half onion too, wash it, and chop.
5. Heat 1 tbsp of olive oil in a pan and put the minced onion to brown.
6. Add the cubed green pepper, stir, and cook for 5 minutes.
7. Now add the cardamom seeds, curry powder, and a cup of water and cook for another 2–3 minutes.
8. Add the cubed plaice fillet, season with salt and pepper, and continue cooking for 10 minutes.
9. As soon as the plaice is cooked, turn it off and set it aside.
10. At this point, the pasta will be cooked.
11. Drain it and put it in the pan with the plaice.
12. Mix until well incorporated, then transfer the pasta and fish to serving plates.
13. Sprinkle with chopped chives and serve this plaice pasta curry dish.

31. Salmon and Tomato Rice

PREPARATION TIME: 15 minutes

COOKING TIME: 40 minutes

CALORIES: 510

NUTRITIONAL VALUES: CARBS: 45 G; PROTEIN: 14 G; FAT: 12 G

INGREDIENTS FOR 2 SERVINGS

- 4.2 oz brown rice
- 3.5 oz smoked salmon
- 1 tsp cumin powder
- 1 tbsp chopped scallion
- 2 tbsp chopped tomatoes
- 1 tbsp chopped garlic
- ½ lime, juice
- Olive oil to taste
- Salt and pepper to taste

DIRECTIONS

1. First, clean and slice the smoked salmon. Then, transfer these slices to a bowl, along with the lime juice, minced garlic, cumin powder, salt, pepper, and a little olive oil.
2. Let the smoked salmon marinate for 10 minutes.
3. Now, arrange some water, salt, and pepper in a saucepan and bring to a boil. Once boiling, cook the rice for 25–30 minutes, then drain it and transfer it to a bowl.
4. Pour a drizzle of oil into a pan and brown the chopped spring onion for a couple of minutes. Add the marinated salmon with all the marinating liquid and chopped tomatoes. Stir and cook for 10 minutes.
5. Put the salmon with all the cooking juices in the bowl with the rice.
6. Put the rice, tomato, and salmon on the serving plates and serve.

32. Zucchini Soup with Fenugreek Seeds and Spring Onion

PREPARATION TIME: 15 minutes

COOKING TIME: 35 minutes

CALORIES: 90

NUTRITIONAL VALUES: CARBS: 11 G; PROTEIN: 4 G; FAT: 4 G

INGREDIENTS FOR 2 SERVINGS

- 2 large size zucchinis
- 2 spring onions
- 14 oz vegetable broth
- 1 tsp minced fenugreek seeds
- 1 tsp fennel seeds
- Salt and pepper to taste
- Olive oil to taste

DIRECTIONS

1. Wash the 2 spring onions and cut them into small pieces.
2. Also wash the zucchini, peel them, and cut them into small pieces.
3. Heat a bit of oil in a pan and then sauté the spring onions.
4. Wait 5 minutes and then add the zucchini.
5. Add salt and pepper and the broth, and cook for another 20 minutes.
6. After 20 minutes, add the fennel and fenugreek seeds, mix, and continue cooking for another 10 minutes.
7. After 10 minutes, turn off and mince everything with an immersion blender.
8. Once you have obtained a thick and smooth soup, distribute equally the cream into 2 plates.
9. Season the zucchinis and spring onions cream with a drizzle of oil and serve.

33. Tilapia, Turmeric, and Almond Cream

PREPARATION TIME: 15 minutes and 30 minutes to rest

COOKING TIME: 45 minutes

CALORIES: 190

NUTRITIONAL VALUES: CARBS: 2 G; PROTEIN: 28 G; FAT: 6 GR

INGREDIENTS FOR 2 SERVINGS

- 7 oz cubed tilapia fillet
- 1 cup sugar-free almond milk
- 1 tsp fennel seeds
- 1 tsp turmeric powder
- 2 tbsp chopped almonds
- Salt and pepper to taste

DIRECTIONS

1. First, wash and cube the tilapia fillet (that you have previously cleaned).
2. Pour the almond milk into a saucepan, add the tilapia fillet, and boil over low heat for about 20 minutes.
3. Once this time has passed, add turmeric powder, fennel seeds, and a pinch of salt and pepper, mix well and cook over low heat for another 10 minutes.
4. Next, transfer the tilapia mixture along with the milk and chopped almonds to the blender, and divide the resulting cream into 2 individual cups.
5. Serve still hot.

34. Spicy Turnips and Shallot Soup

PREPARATION TIME: 20 minutes

COOKING TIME: 25 minutes

CALORIES: 80

NUTRITIONAL VALUES: CARBS: 10 G; PROTEIN: 3 G; FAT: 2 G

INGREDIENTS FOR 2 SERVINGS

- 7 oz turnips
- 1 shallot, chopped
- ¼ cup vegetable broth
- 2 tsp cumin powder
- 2 tsp turmeric powder
- 1 tbsp olive oil
- 1 tsp ground cinnamon
- Salt and pepper to taste

DIRECTIONS

1. As the first step, wash the turnips and cut them into pieces.
2. Put the chopped shallot and oil in a pan and fry for 2 minutes.
3. Add the cumin, turmeric, and ground cinnamon, and mix.
4. Now add the turnips and cook, stirring constantly for 5 minutes.
5. Add the salt and pepper and coat everything with the vegetable stock. Arrange the lid to the pan and cook for 15 minutes.
6. After cooking, turn off the heat and blend the shallot and turnips with an immersion blender.
7. Pour the turnips spicy soup into two plates, season with very little oil, and serve.

35. Zucchini Stuffed With Smoked Salmon and Soy Cheese

PREPARATION TIME: 25 minutes

COOKING TIME: 20 minutes

CALORIES: 270

NUTRITIONAL VALUES: CARBS: 5 G; PROTEIN: 16 G; FAT: 12 G

INGREDIENTS FOR 2SERVINGS

- 2 large size zucchinis
- 3.5 oz smoked salmon
- 2.5 oz soy cheese
- 1 tsp chopped jalapeno
- 1 tsp pink peppercorns
- 1 tbsp chopped scallion
- 2 tbsp chopped peppers
- Salt and pepper to taste
- Olive oil to taste

DIRECTIONS

1. Start by peeling and washing both the zucchinis and then split them in half lengthwise.
2. Then, helping with a spoon, scoop out their pulp and place it directly in the blender glass.
3. Pat dry the soy cheese and then cut it into pieces.
4. Put the chopped peppers, chopped jalapeno, pink peppercorns, and cheese in the glass of the blender.
5. Add salt, pepper, and a bit of olive oil, and blend everything at maximum speed.
6. Pour the just obtained mixture into a bowl, add the smoked salmon, and cover.

7. Now, brush a baking sheet with a little olive oil and arrange the zucchini inside.

8. Fill the zucchinis with the salmon-jalapeno-cheese mixture and transfer to the oven.

9. Cook the just-filled zucchini at 392°F for about 20 minutes.

10. When done, let the stuffed zucchini cool slightly, sprinkle some chopped scallion on top and serve.

Main Course Dishes

36. Almond and Pepper Turkey

PREPARATION TIME: 20 minutes

COOKING TIME: 20 minutes

CALORIES: 305

NUTRITIONAL VALUES: CARBS: 8 G; PROTEIN: 53 G; FAT: 9 G

INGREDIENTS FOR 2 SERVINGS

- 2 turkey breasts (7 oz each)
- ½ cup almond milk
- 1 yellow pepper
- 1 white onion
- Juice of 1 lemon
- 1 tbsp olive oil
- Salt and pepper to taste

DIRECTIONS

1. As the first step, peel the onion and cut it into thin slices.

2. Wash the pepper and cut it into slices too.

3. Remove the fat from the turkey and brown it for 2 minutes in a pan with hot olive oil.

4. Flip the turkey, add the onions and pepper, and cook for another 2 minutes.

5. Now add the lemon juice, almond milk, salt, and pepper and cook for 8 minutes.

6. Next, put the lid on the pan and keep on cooking for another 7 minutes.

7. After 7 minutes, switch off and put the turkey and peppers on the plates.

8. Sprinkle with the cooking sauce and serve this anti-inflammatory dish.

37. Avocado and Herbs Sauce Tilapia

PREPARATION TIME: 15 minutes

COOKING TIME: 10 minutes

CALORIES: 360

NUTRITIONAL VALUES: CARBS: 7 G; PROTEIN: 25 G; FAT: 20 G

INGREDIENTS FOR 2 SERVINGS

- 2 fresh tilapia fillets, 7 oz each
- 1 ripe avocado
- 10 mint leaves
- 6 sage leaves
- 2 tbsp already chopped pecans
- Chia seeds
- Olive oil to taste
- Salt and pepper to taste

DIRECTIONS

1. Start this anti-inflammatory recipe, by preparing the sauce. Put the sage and mint leaves, pecans, salt, pepper, and 2 tbsp of olive oil in a blender and mince everything.
2. Meanwhile, clean and wash the tilapia fillets and transfer them to a pan with a drizzle of hot oil.
3. Cook the tilapia fillets for 3–4 minutes on each side; the fish must only be seared, not overcooked.
4. Once ready, place the tilapia fillets on a cutting board, sprinkle them with the chia seeds, and then cut them into slices.
5. Peel, pit, and take the avocado pulp, divide it into thin slices and distribute it into 2 plates.
6. Put the tilapia slices on top, sprinkle with the herbs and pecan sauce, and serve.

38. Broccoli and Tuna Chipotle Stew

PREPARATION TIME: 25 minutes

COOKING TIME: 20 minutes

CALORIES: 260

NUTRITIONAL VALUES: CARBS: 7 G; PROTEIN: 24 G; FAT: 11 G

INGREDIENTS FOR 2 SERVINGS

- 7 oz tuna fillet
- 1 sliced scallion
- 7 oz broccoli
- 2 sage leaves
- 2 cups fish stock
- 1 tsp chopped chipotle
- 1 tsp chopped chives
- Salt and pepper to taste
- Olive oil to taste

DIRECTIONS

1. Wash the sage leaves and put them in a pan.
2. Add the scallion cut into slices and a drizzle of oil and heat everything up.
3. Now add the fish stock and bring it to a boil.
4. Next, rinse the broccoli under running water, separate the florets, cut them into small pieces, and put them in the pot with the boiling fish stock.
5. Cook for another 5 minutes, then add the cleaned diced tuna fillet.
6. Season with salt and pepper, add the chipotle, put the lid on, and cook for 15 minutes.
7. After 15 minutes, turn off and pour the stew on 2 plates, covering it with the cooking juices and chopped chives.
8. Now you can serve this anti-inflammatory stew.

39. Cashew and Zucchini-Crusted Salmon

PREPARATION TIME: 25 minutes

COOKING TIME: 12 minutes

CALORIES: 340

NUTRITIONAL VALUES: CARBS: 9 G; PROTEIN: 30 G; FAT: 18 G

INGREDIENTS FOR 2 SERVINGS

- 14 oz cleaned salmon fillet
- 2 tbsp cashews
- 1 tsp minced chili pepper
- 1 zucchini
- Salt and pepper to taste
- Olive oil to taste

DIRECTIONS

1. As the first step, mince finely the cashews.
2. Clean and brush the salmon fillet with olive oil.
3. Peel and wash the zucchini and slice in a diagonal way.
4. Sprinkle the salmon fillet with salt, pepper, chopped cashews, and finally with chopped chili pepper.
5. Place a sheet of parchment paper in a baking pan and place the salmon fillet on top.
6. Cover the salmon with sliced zucchini and season again with oil, salt, and pepper.
7. Arrange the baking pan in the oven and bake at 375°F for 10 minutes.
8. After cooking time, remove the fish from the oven and slice it into many small slices.
9. Put the covered salmon slices on 2 plates and serve.

40. Cilantro Trout and Tomato

PREPARATION TIME: 15 minutes

COOK TIME: 20–25 minutes

CALORIES: 230

NUTRITIONAL VALUES: CARBS: 10 G; PROTEIN: 20 G; FAT: 11 G

INGREDIENTS FOR 2 SERVINGS

- 14 oz trout fillet
- 1 scallion
- 1 tsp freshly chopped cilantro leaves
- 7 oz cherry tomatoes
- 1 tsp turmeric powder
- 2 tbsp pitted and chopped green olives
- ½ cup fresh sugar-free lime juice
- Olive oil to taste
- Salt and pepper to taste

DIRECTIONS

1. First, clean, remove the bone, wash, and slice the trout. Let it drain for a few minutes.
2. Peel the scallion too, wash it, and then chop it.
3. Take a baking pan, line it with a little oil, and lay the slices of trout on top.
4. Drizzle with oil and sprinkle with the chopped scallion.
5. Next, wash the cherry tomatoes too, dry and cut them in half.

6. Spread the cherry tomatoes over the trout slices and sprinkle with salt, turmeric powder, pepper, and freshly chopped cilantro leaves.

7. Finally, add the pitted and chopped green olives to the trout.

8. Place the pan inside the preheated oven to 338°F and cook for about 18 minutes.

9. After 8 minutes, flip the trout, drizzle with lime juice, and cook for another 10 minutes.

10. Serve this dish while still hot.

41. Coconut and Amchoor Chicken

PREPARATION TIME: 35 minutes

COOKING TIME: 15 minutes

CALORIES: 390

NUTRITIONAL VALUES: CARBS: 5 G; PROTEIN: 52 G; FAT: 10 G

INGREDIENTS FOR 2 SERVINGS

- 14 oz chicken breast
- 1 tsp amchoor powder
- 1 tsp freshly grated ginger
- ½ cup coconut milk
- 1 tbsp apple cider vinegar
- 1 shallot
- 1 tbsp chopped fresh thyme
- 1 tbsp oil
- 1 tsp salt
- ½ tsp chopped jalapeno

DIRECTIONS

1. First, put salt, chopped jalapeno, amchoor, and vinegar in a bowl and mix everything with a fork.
2. Put the chicken breast on a chopping board, remove the fat excess, and divide it into 4 slices. Transfer the chicken slices to a plate.
3. Spread the amchoor and jalapeno marinade on top of the chicken and marinate for 15 minutes.
4. Heat the oil in a pan together with the peeled shallot and fresh ginger.
5. Add the coconut milk and thyme and bring to a boil.
6. Boil for 5 minutes, then add the chicken marinated slices.
7. Cover the pan with a lid and cook for 15–20 minutes.
8. When the coconut and amchoor chicken is cooked, turn them off and put them on 2 plates. Drizzle with the delicious sauce on top and serve.

42. Cumin, Honey, and Chia Seeds Chicken

PREPARATION TIME: 10 minutes

COOKING TIME: 20 minutes

CALORIES: 400

NUTRITIONAL VALUES: CARBS: 12 G; PROTEIN: 52 G; FAT: 9 G

INGREDIENTS FOR 2 SERVINGS

- 2 chicken breasts (7 oz each)
- 2 tsp chia seeds
- 2 tbsp raw honey
- Juice of 1 lime
- 2 tsp soy sauce
- 1 tsp cumin powder
- Salt and pepper to taste
- Olive oil to taste

DIRECTIONS

1. As the first step, mix the honey with the lime juice, 1 tbsp olive oil, the soy sauce, the cumin powder, and a pinch of salt and pepper in a bowl.
2. Put the cleaned chicken breast in a baking dish and cover it with the sauce. Marinate for 20 minutes at least, turning the chicken occasionally.
3. After this time, sprinkle the chicken with the chia seeds.
4. Place the baking pan in the oven and cook at 392°F for 20 minutes.
5. After 20 minutes, take the chicken out of the oven and put it on 2 plates.
6. Sprinkle the chicken with the rest of the lime and cumin sauce that remained in the bottom of the baking dish and serve.

43. Kale and Smoked Salmon Eggs

PREPARATION TIME: 10 minutes

COOKING TIME: 12 minutes

CALORIES: 190

NUTRITIONAL VALUES: CARBS: 4 G; PROTEIN: 18 G; FAT: 10 G

INGREDIENTS FOR 2 SERVINGS

- 2 large size eggs
- 3.5 oz kale leaves
- 2.5 oz thinly sliced smoked salmon
- 1 tsp turmeric powder
- 1 tbsp olive oil
- Salt and pepper to taste

DIRECTIONS

1. As the first step for this recipe, wash and dry the kale leaves, then chop.
2. Next, put a non-stick pan to heat with the olive oil.
3. Once hot, add the chopped kale and brown it for 4 minutes, seasoning with salt and pepper and turmeric powder. Leave to cook for another 2 minutes.
4. In a dish, lightly batter the 2 eggs, and after 5 minutes, put the eggs in the pan with the kale.
5. Add the thinly sliced smoked salmon and stir constantly so that the eggs will be split into many separate pieces.
6. Keep on cooking for 5 minutes and then transfer the salmon-kale eggs to a serving dish.
7. Serve this anti-inflammatory recipe still hot.

44. Tuna Brown Rice and Pecans Poke Bowl

PREPARATION TIME: 10 minutes

COOKING TIME: 20 minutes

CALORIES: 435

NUTRITIONAL VALUES: CARBS: 41 G; PROTEIN: 15 G; FAT: 18 GS

INGREDIENTS FOR 2 SERVINGS

- 3.5 oz brown rice
- 1 ripe avocado
- 2.5 oz drained tuna in oil
- 1.8 oz chopped mango
- 2 tsp chopped pecans
- Lemon juice to taste
- Olive oil to taste
- Salt and pepper to taste

DIRECTIONS

1. Start preparing this anti-inflammatory tuna poke bowl by cooking the rice. Let boil in salted water for the time indicated on the package.
2. Once the brown rice is ready, drain and let it cool under running water.
3. Peel the avocado, remove the stone, wash it, dry it, and then divide it into cubes.
4. Do the same with the mango.
5. Put the rice in a bowl and then place the avocado and mango cubes and chopped drained tuna next to it.
6. Season with olive oil, lemon juice, salt, and pepper, sprinkle with chopped walnuts, and serve this delicious poke bowl.

45. Mint and Garam Masala Baked Halibut

PREPARATION TIME: 10 minutes

COOKING TIME: 5 minutes

CALORIES: 190

NUTRITIONAL VALUES: CARBS: 2 G; PROTEIN: 24 G; FAT: 10 G

INGREDIENTS FOR 2 SERVINGS

- 7 oz halibut fillet
- 1 tbsp olive oil
- 1 tbsp fresh mint, chopped
- 1 tsp garam masala
- 1 tsp orange zest
- Salt and pepper to taste

DIRECTIONS

1. First, rinse the already cleaned halibut and let it dry, then slice.
2. Next, season the halibut slices with salt and pepper.
3. Add the garam masala and chopped mint to the sliced fish.
4. Place the fish slices in a baking tray and sprinkle them with olive oil and the orange zest on top.
5. Bake at 392°F for 12–13 minutes.
6. Serve this halibut anti-inflammatory dish still hot.

46. Mushrooms and Cucumber Plaice

PREPARATION TIME: 25 minutes

COOKING TIME: 12 minutes

CALORIES: 250

NUTRITIONAL VALUES: CARBS: 7 G; PROTEIN: 26 G; FAT: 6 G

INGREDIENTS FOR 2 SERVINGS

- 14 oz plaice fillet
- 10.5 oz button mushrooms
- ½ cucumber
- 1 scallion
- 1 tbsp chopped cilantro
- Salt and pepper to taste
- 1 tbsp olive oil

DIRECTIONS

1. Start by getting rid of the stem and clean the button mushrooms well by removing all the earthy parts, then cut them into slices.
2. Peel the scallion and cut it into slices.
3. Peel the cucumber and cut it into slices, too.
4. Then, line a baking pan with olive oil.
5. Remove the skin from the plaice, cut it into 4 slices, and put it in the baking pan.
6. Place the cucumber pieces in the baking pan with the fish.
7. Add the sliced mushrooms and season with oil, salt, and pepper. Sprinkle with the cilantro and scallion and place the plaice in the oven. Bake at 392°F for 12 minutes, turning the place halfway through cooking.
8. After 12 minutes, remove the plaice from the oven and arrange it on 2 plates.
9. Add the mushroom slices and cucumber, and serve.

47. Peas and Zucchini Salmon

PREPARATION TIME: 20 minutes

COOKING TIME: 15 minutes

CALORIES: 410

NUTRITIONAL VALUES: CARBS: 22 G; PROTEIN: 38 G; FAT: 12 G

INGREDIENTS FOR 2 SERVINGS

- 2 salmon fillets, 7 oz each
- 3.5 oz fresh-shelled peas
- ½ zucchini
- 1 pinch of cumin powder
- 2 tbsp vegetable stock
- Salt and pepper to taste
- Olive oil to taste

DIRECTIONS

1. As the first step, wash the salmon and pat it dry with a paper towel, then divide the fillets into 4 parts.
2. Heat a bit of oil in a pan and then put the salmon fillets in. Cook for 2 minutes on each side.
3. Wash the zucchini, cube it, and put it in the pan with the salmon.
4. Add the peas to the salmon, which you have previously rinsed with running water, and season with salt, cumin powder, and pepper.
5. Add the hot vegetable stock and cook for 10 minutes, checking the cooking and stirring occasionally.
6. After 10 minutes, turn off the heat and divide the salmon between 2 plates, along with the peas and zucchini, and serve.

48. Pumpkin and Olives Turkey

PREPARATION TIME: 45 minutes

COOKING TIME: 30 minutes

CALORIES: 350

NUTRITIONAL VALUES: CARBS: 2 G; PROTEIN: G; FAT: 10 G

INGREDIENTS FOR 2 SERVINGS

- 2 turkey breasts (7 oz each)
- 7 oz pumpkin
- 2 tbsp black olives
- 1 tsp ginger powder
- 1 tsp cumin powder
- Juice of ½ lime
- Salt and pepper to taste
- Olive oil to taste

DIRECTIONS

1. Put the already cleaned turkey breasts in a bowl and season with the lime juice, ginger, salt, pepper, and oil, and leave to marinate for 20 minutes.
2. Meanwhile, remove the peel and seeds from the pumpkin and divide it into slices.
3. Pit and chop the olives.
4. Brush a baking pan with olive oil and put the pumpkin inside.
5. Toss the pumpkin with oil, salt, cumin powder, and pepper and place in the oven to cook at 356° F for 20 minutes.
6. After 20 minutes, take the baking pan out of the oven and add the turkey and olives.
7. Place again in the oven and cook for another 10 minutes.
8. After cooking, take the turkey and pumpkin baking pan out of the oven. Put the turkey, olives, and pumpkin on 2 plates and serve.

49. Rosemary and Pine Nuts Crusted Turkey

PREPARATION TIME: 20 minutes

COOKING TIME: 10 minutes

CALORIES: 270

NUTRITIONAL VALUES: CARBS: 3 G; PROTEIN: 39 G; FAT: 8 G

INGREDIENTS FOR 2 SERVINGS

- 10.5 oz turkey breast
- 2 oz pine nuts
- 1 tbsp fresh rosemary, chopped
- 2 tbsp olive oil, divided
- 2 tbsp panko
- Salt and pepper to taste

DIRECTIONS

1. Put the panko into a bowl and add the chopped rosemary, salt, pepper, and 1 tbsp oil.
2. Chop the pine nuts finely and put them in the bowl with the rosemary panko.
3. Mix all the ingredients well until you get a consistency of wet sand.
4. Take the cleaned turkey breast and coat it entirely with the breading.
5. Heat a pan with the remaining 1 tbsp oil and cook the turkey breast for 6–7 minutes on each side.
6. Once cooked, turn off the heat and cut the turkey into slices.
7. Put the turkey slices on 2 plates and serve.

50. Zucchini and Alaska Pollock Spicy Soup

PREPARATION TIME: 15 minutes

COOKING TIME: 20 minutes

CALORIES: 210

NUTRITIONAL VALUES: CARBS: 7 G; PROTEIN: 26 G; FAT: 12 G

INGREDIENTS FOR 2SERVINGS

- 14 oz zucchinis
- 7 oz cleaned and cubed Alaska Pollock fillet
- 1 red onion
- 2 tsp freshly chopped coriander
- 1 sprig of chopped cilantro
- 1 tsp chopped rosemary
- 1 chipotle
- ¼ cup water
- Salt and pepper to taste
- Olive oil to taste

DIRECTIONS

1. Peel and wash the red onion, and then slice thinly.
2. Wash and dry the chipotle and chop it as well.
3. Next, trim the zucchini, wash them, and cut them into cubes.
4. Now, pour 2 tbsp oil into the pan.
5. When is hot enough, brown the red onion and fresh herbs (rosemary, cilantro, and coriander).
6. Add the zucchini and chopped chipotle and sauté for 10 minutes.
7. Then, season with salt and pepper, add ¼ cup of water, and keep on cooking for another 15 minutes.
8. Rinse the cleaned Alaska Pollock fillet and cube it.
9. Arrange the cubed fish in the pan with herbs and zucchini.
10. Cook for another 10–12 minutes.
11. Turn off, put the spicy Alaska Pollock and zucchini soup on serving plates, and serve.

Vegetarian Dishes

51. Broccoli and Cumin Tofu Croquettes

PREPARATION TIME: 10 minutes

COOKING TIME: 20 minutes

CALORIES: 180

NUTRITIONAL VALUES: CARBS: 7 G; PROTEIN: 22 G; FAT: 10 G

INGREDIENTS FOR 2 SERVINGS

- 3.5 oz tofu cheese
- ½ broccoli
- 1 pinch of baking soda
- 2 tbsp wholemeal flour
- ½ tsp cumin powder
- 1 scallion
- Salt and pepper to taste
- Olive oil to taste

DIRECTIONS

1. First, take the tofu and divide it into pieces.

2. Meanwhile, wash the half broccoli and cut the florets.

3. Peel, wash, and chop the scallion too.

4. Sauté the broccoli florets and the chopped spring onion with a drop of oil and a pinch of salt and, once golden, cover with a lid and cook for about 15 minutes until very soft.

5. Then turn off the heat and let chill.

6. Blend the softened broccoli in the food processor until you get some fine crumbs.

7. Then add tofu cheese along with the baking soda, cumin powder, and flour.

8. Grind the ingredients well with the help of a spoon until it forms a fairly firm mixture.

9. Grasp a little portion of the tofu and broccoli dough and create a croquette shape, gradually placing them on a baking sheet.

10. Brush them with a bit of olive oil and cook them in a hot oven at 392°F for 15–20 minutes, or until golden.

11. Now you can serve your vegetarian anti-inflammatory croquettes.

52. Kale and Soy Cheese Curry Cream

PREPARATION TIME: 20 minutes

COOKING TIME: 10–15 minutes

CALORIES: 180

NUTRITIONAL VALUES: CARBS: 2 G; PROTEIN: 16 G; FAT: 7 G

INGREDIENTS FOR 2SERVINGS

- 3.5 oz soy cheese
- 7 oz cooked kale leaves
- 1 cup hot vegetable stock
- ¼ white onion
- 1 tsp curry powder
- 1 tsp tomato puree
- Salt and pepper to taste
- Olive oil to taste

DIRECTIONS

1. The first thing to do is to peel and chop the onion.
2. Next, take a pan and heat some oil.
3. Brown the onion for 2 minutes, add the boiled kale leaves, and stir well.
4. Now add the vegetable stock, bring it to a boil, and then keep on cooking for another 9–10 minutes.
5. Take out of the heat, blend the kale with an immersion blender, put back on the heat, and add the tomato puree and curry powder.
6. Season with salt and pepper, then place the kale cream on serving plates.
7. Meanwhile, cut the soy cheese into pieces.
8. Put the pieces of soy cheese over the kale and curry cream, season with a drizzle of oil, and serve.

53. Peas, Lime, and Jalapeno Cream

PREPARATION TIME: 5 minutes

COOKING TIME: 10 minutes

CALORIES: 170

NUTRITIONAL VALUES: CARBS: 12 G; PROTEIN: 15 G; FAT: 3 G

INGREDIENTS FOR 2 SERVINGS

- 2.3 oz fresh peas
- Juice of 2 limes
- 1 tsp chopped cilantro leaves
- 1 tsp chopped jalapeno
- Salt and pepper to taste
- Olive oil to taste

DIRECTIONS

1. Start by rinsing the fresh peas under running water and letting them drain.
2. Then, bring a pot of water and salt to a boil. Once it's boiling, let the peas cook for 10 minutes.
3. After 10 minutes, drain and then transfer it to the glass of the blender.
4. Add the chopped jalapeño, olive oil, salt, pepper, and the filtered juice of the 2 lemons to the blender and begin to blend everything at high speed until you have a thick and homogeneous cream.
5. Pour the cream into 2 serving bowls, sprinkle with chopped cilantro, and serve.

54. Pepper, Cucumber, and Zucchini Salad

PREPARATION TIME: 10 minutes

COOKING TIME: 15 minutes

CALORIES: 170

NUTRITIONAL VALUES: CARBS: 12 G; PROTEIN: 14 G; FAT: 5 G

INGREDIENTS FOR 2 SERVINGS

- 2 zucchinis
- ½ scallion
- ½ bell pepper
- 1 cucumber
- ½ tsp turmeric powder
- ⅓ cup low-fat white yogurt
- 1 tsp apple cider vinegar
- 3 tsp olive oil
- 1 tsp fresh minced oregano
- Sal to taste

DIRECTIONS

1. Start by preparing the yogurt dressing for the salad. Take the blender glass and add the white yogurt, turmeric powder, vinegar, and a pinch of salt and blend.

2. Pour in the olive oil and keep on mixing.

3. Let the yogurt and turmeric cream rest in the refrigerator for 40 minutes.

4. Now move on to preparing the zucchini and cucumber. Peel and wash both and cut them into small slices.

5. Sauté these slices in a pan with olive oil for about 10–15 minutes, until they are soft.

6. After this time, drain both the zucchini and cucumber and let them cool completely.

7. In the meantime, wash the bell pepper, remove all seeds, and slice.

8. Peel the spring onion and slice it finely too,

9. Add the sliced vegetables to the zucchini and cucumber, season with a pinch of salt, and add the yogurt sauce.

10. Sprinkle with the oregano, mix, and serve immediately.

55. Tomatoes with Ginger-Vinegar Sauce

PREPARATION TIME: 15 minutes

COOKING TIME: 8 minutes

CALORIES: 50

NUTRITIONAL VALUES: CARBS: 3 G; PROTEIN: 1 G; FAT: 2 G

INGREDIENTS FOR 2 SERVINGS

- 7 oz tomatoes
- 1 garlic clove
- 1 tsp powdered ginger
- 1 sprig of chopped coriander
- 3 tbsp apple cider vinegar
- Salt and pepper to taste
- Olive oil to taste

DIRECTIONS

1. Start by washing the tomatoes, then cut them in half.
2. Brush the halved tomatoes with olive oil and season with salt and pepper.
3. Heat a grill and put the halved tomatoes.
4. Cook the tomatoes for 3 minutes per side.
5. Once done, remove the tomatoes from the grill and place them on a serving dish.
6. Peel and wash the garlic and then divide it into thin slices.
7. At this point, sprinkle the tomatoes with the garlic and chopped coriander.
8. Now, to prepare the sauce, add the vinegar, 2 tsp oil, ginger powder, salt, and pepper to a bowl.
9. Drizzle the tomatoes with the just prepared sauce and serve.

Gluten-Free Recipes

56. Chipotle, Chickpeas, and Spinach Mint Cream

PREPARATION TIME: 15 minutes

CALORIES: 200

NUTRITIONAL VALUES: CARBS: 34 G; PROTEIN: 12 G; FAT: 3 G

INGREDIENTS FOR 2 SERVINGS

- 2.3 oz already boiled chickpeas
- 3.5 oz boiled spinach
- 1 tsp chopped mint leaves
- 1 tsp chopped chipotle
- Salt and pepper to taste
- Olive oil to taste

DIRECTIONS

1. Start by rinsing the boiled chickpeas under running water and letting them drain.
2. Do the same with the spinach.

3. After having drained both, transfer to the blender glass.

4. Add the chopped chipotle, olive oil, salt, pepper, and mint leaves to the blender.

5. Then, start to mince everything at high speed until you have a thick and homogeneous cream.

6. Pour the spinach and chickpeas cream into 2 serving bowls and serve.

57. Mango, Avocado, and Nuts Salad

PREPARATION TIME: 15 minutes

CALORIES: 280

NUTRITIONAL VALUES: CARBS: 12 G; PROTEIN: 14 G; FAT: 18 G

INGREDIENTS FOR 2 SERVINGS

- 1 mango
- ½ red onion
- ½ avocado
- 2 tsp mixed nuts
- ½ tsp ginger powder
- 1 tsp honey
- ⅓ cup low-fat white yogurt
- 1 tsp fresh orange juice
- 2 tsp olive oil, divided
- Salt to taste

DIRECTIONS

1. Begin this recipe by preparing the dressing for the salad. Take the blender glass and add the low-fat yogurt, ginger powder, orange juice, and a pinch of salt, and start blending.
2. Add 1 tsp of olive oil and honey and keep on mixing.
3. Let the yogurt and orange cream rest in the refrigerator for 20 minutes.
4. Now move on to preparing avocado and mango. Peel, pit, and wash both and cut them into small cubes.
5. Peel the red onion and slice it finely.

6. Add the freshly cut fruit and onion to a bowl, season with a pinch of salt, and pour the dressing on top.

7. Sprinkle with the chopped nuts, mix, and serve immediately.

58. Garlic and Zucchini Curry Tofu Soup

PREPARATION TIME: 20 minutes

COOKING TIME: 50 minutes

CALORIES: 190

NUTRITIONAL VALUES: CARBS: 4 G; PROTEIN: 25 G; FAT: 10 G

INGREDIENTS FOR 2 SERVINGS

- 7 oz cubed tofu
- 1 little size zucchini
- 2 garlic cloves
- 1 tsp curry powder
- 2 sage leaves
- 1 sprig of thyme
- 2 cups water
- Salt and pepper to taste
- Olive oil to taste

DIRECTIONS

1. First, peel the zucchini, wash it, and then cut it into cubes.

2. Peel the garlic cloves and then mince.

3. Wash and dry both the sage leaves and thyme.

4. Heat 2 tsp olive oil in a saucepan.

5. Once is hot enough, sauté the minced garlic and zucchini for 5 minutes.

6. Now add the thyme and sage leaves and mix. Add the curry powder too and stir.

7. Cook for a couple of minutes and then add the tofu cubes.

8. Sauté for 2 minutes and then add 2 cups of water.

9. Bring everything to a boil, adding salt and pepper.

10. Lower the heat and keep on cooking the tofu soup for another 10 minutes.

11. After cooking, turn off and pour the garlic zucchini and tofu soup onto 2 plates and serve.

59. Tomato, Radicchio, and Hake Salad

PREPARATION TIME: 15 minutes

COOKING TIME: 15 minutes

CALORIES: 280

NUTRITIONAL VALUES: CARBS: 9 G; PROTEIN: 26 G; FAT: 4 G

INGREDIENTS FOR 2 SERVINGS

- 9 oz hake fillet
- 3.5 oz radicchio
- 6 cherry tomatoes
- 3 tsp apple cider vinegar
- 1 tsp chopped coriander
- 2 bay leaves
- ½ cup water
- Salt and pepper to taste

DIRECTIONS

1. The first step for this recipe is to wash and dry the bay leaves and coriander.
2. Take the hake fillet, remove any bone, and then wash it under running water.
3. Next, dry the fish fillet and halve it.
4. Take a pot, add ½ cup of water and a pinch of salt, and bring to a boil. Then put a steamer basket on top and place the hake, bay leaves, and cilantro inside the basket.
5. Boil for 15 minutes, remembering to add salt and pepper to the fish.
6. After the boiling time, turn it off and let the fish cool.
7. Meanwhile, wash and dry the chicory leaves and chop them finely.
8. Also, wash and dry the cherry tomatoes and cut them in half.
9. Next, in a salad bowl, add the vegetables and a pinch of salt and mix.
10. Take the room-temperature hake and cut it into cubes.
11. Arrange the hake cubes in the salad bowl along with the tomatoes and radicchio.
12. Season this anti-inflammatory salad with olive oil, apple cider vinegar, salt, and pepper, and serve.

60. Zucchini, Cucumber, and Egg Salad

PREPARATION TIME: 10 minutes

COOKING TIME: 20 minutes

CALORIES: 130

NUTRITIONAL VALUES: CARBS: 7 G PROTEIN: 8 G FAT: 12 G

INGREDIENTS FOR 2 SERVINGS

- 7 oz zucchini
- 2 eggs
- 1 cucumber
- 2 cherry tomatoes
- Juice of 1 lemon
- 1 tbsp mustard
- 1 tsp mustard seeds
- Apple cider vinegar to taste
- Olive oil to taste
- Salt and Pepper to taste

DIRECTIONS

1. Begin this gluten-free recipe by cooking the eggs. To do this, pour the eggs directly into a saucepan water fully and let them cook for about 8 minutes from boiling.
2. Once boiled, let them cool, peel them, and cut them into wedges.
3. Now you can move on to the zucchini and cucumber. Wash the cucumber and zucchini and cut them into cubes.
4. Also, wash the cherry tomatoes and cut them into wedges.
5. In a small bowl, add the lemon juice along with the mustard, mustard seeds, and a splash of apple cider vinegar.
6. Stir well, also adding a pinch of salt.
7. Arrange the eggs, cucumbers, tomatoes, and zucchini on 2 plates, top with the lemon-vinegar emulsion, and serve.

Snack Recipes

61. Peaches in Orange, Cinnamon, and Coconut Syrup

PREPARATION TIME: 15 minutes

COOKING TIME: 30 minutes

CALORIES: 150

NUTRITIONAL VALUES: CARBS: 25 G; PROTEIN: 2 G; FAT: 1 G

INGREDIENTS FOR 2 SERVINGS

- 2 small peaches
- 1 orange
- 2 tsp honey
- 4 tbsp water
- 1 tsp ground cinnamon
- 1 tbsp coconut flour (divided)

DIRECTIONS

1. First, peel the peaches, pit, slice, and put the slices in a pan.

2. Then, wash the orange, peel it, and put the peel in the peach pan together with its juice.

3. Add ground cinnamon, honey, and 4 tbsp water.

4. Cook the orange syrup peaches for 30 minutes, then remove and place them in 2 plates.

5. Sprinkle the peaches with the coconut flour and orange-cinnamon syrup and serve.

62. Pineapple with Ginger-Pomegranate Cream

PREPARATION TIME: 20 minutes

COOKING TIME: 10 minutes

CALORIES: 80

NUTRITIONAL VALUES: CARBS: 12 G; PROTEIN: 3 G; FAT: 2 G

INGREDIENTS FOR 2 SERVINGS

- ½ pineapple
- 2 tsp pomegranate juice
- 1 tsp fresh minced ginger
- 1 cup low-fat white yogurt
- 2 tsp honey

DIRECTIONS

1. As the first step, peel the pineapple and cut the pulp into slices.
2. Place parchment paper on a baking sheet and top with the freshly cut pineapple.
3. Next, cook the pineapple in the oven at 392°F for 8–9 minutes.
4. Meanwhile, put the low-fat yogurt, honey, fresh minced ginger, and pomegranate juice in a bowl. Stir all these ingredients until you get a smooth and homogeneous cream.
5. After the cooking time in the oven, remove the pineapple and let it cool for 5 minutes.
6. After the cooling time, distribute the baked pineapple on 2 plates, cover it with the pomegranate and ginger cream, and serve.

63. Oatmeal with Mango and Berries Cream

PREPARATION TIME: 20 minutes

DIFFICULTY LEVEL: Easy

CALORIES: 150

NUTRITIONAL VALUES: CARBS: 14 G; PROTEIN: 10 G; FAT: 7 G

INGREDIENTS FOR 2 SERVINGS

- 1.8 oz low-fat yogurt
- 1 ripe mango
- 2 tbsp mixed berries
- 2 tsp chopped pecans
- 2 tbsp oat flakes
- Lime juice to taste

DIRECTIONS

1. The first thing to do is to peel the mango, pit, and slice.
2. Put the mango slices in the blender and add the lime juice and the previously washed mixed berries.
3. Turn on the blender and blend everything for 10 seconds.
4. Now add the chopped pecans and continue mixing until you get a homogeneous and smooth cream.
5. Pour the oat flakes into the bottom of 2 cups, add the mango and walnut cream, and serve.

64. Pineapple, Plum, and Orange Juice

PREPARATION TIME: 15 minutes

CALORIES: 180

NUTRITIONAL VALUES: CARBS: 25 G; PROTEIN: 2 G; FAT: 0 G

INGREDIENTS FOR 2 SERVINGS

- 3.5 oz pineapple pulp
- 2 plums
- 1 cup fresh sugar-free orange juice
- 1 tsp vanilla extract
- 1 pinch of ground cinnamon
- 4 ice cubes
- 1 tsp honey

DIRECTIONS

1. As the first step, wash and pat dry the pineapple pulp and then cut it into pieces.
2. Pit the plums, wash, and cut them into pieces too.
3. Put the plums and pineapple in the blender glass along with the vanilla, the pinch of cinnamon, and honey.
4. Mince everything for a few seconds and then add the orange juice.
5. Blend again for 20 seconds and finally add the ice cubes.
6. Keep blending until you get a thick and creamy mixture.
7. Pour this anti-inflammatory juice into 2 glasses and serve.

65. Vanilla and Pistachio Pudding

PREPARATION TIME: 5 minutes

COOKING TIME: 5 minutes

CALORIES: 150

NUTRITIONAL VALUES: CARBS: 7 G; PROTEIN: 6 G; FAT: 14 G

INGREDIENTS FOR 2 SERVINGS

- 3 tbsp chopped pistachios
- 1 tbsp coconut flour
- 3 tbsp water
- 1 tbsp coconut milk
- 1 tbsp low-fat yogurt
- 1 tsp vanilla extract
- 2 tsp honey

DIRECTIONS

1. To start this recipe, you must put all the ingredients in a microwave-safe container and mix very well.

2. Put in the microwave and cook for 1 minute.

3. Your super easy pudding is now ready to serve.

Smoothie Recipes

66. Apricot, Banana, and Ginger Smoothie

PREPARATION TIME: 15 minutes

CALORIES: 200

NUTRITIONAL VALUES: CARBS: 31 G; PROTEIN: 8 G; FAT: 4 G

INGREDIENTS FOR 2 SERVINGS

- 1 banana
- 3 apricots
- 0.2 oz ginger
- 1 cup coconut milk
- 1 tsp vanilla extract
- 4 ice cubes

DIRECTIONS

1. Start by peeling the banana and cutting it into slices.
2. Peel the apricots too, pit, wash them and cut them into small pieces.
3. Mince finely the ginger root.
4. Put the ginger and the fruit in the glass of the blender and blend for about 40 seconds.
5. Next, add the vanilla and coconut milk to the mixture and blend for another 30 seconds.
6. Now add the ice too and mince until you get a very thick smoothie.
7. Finally, pour the smoothie into 2 separate glasses, add the straws, and serve.

67. Avocado and Kiwi Smoothie

PREPARATION TIME: 10 minutes

CALORIES: 260

NUTRITIONAL VALUES: CARBS: 8 G; PROTEIN: 8 G; FAT: 19 G

INGREDIENTS FOR 2 SERVINGS

- 1 cup sugar-free vegetable milk
- 1 avocado
- 1 kiwi
- 2 oz ice
- 2 tsp chopped hazelnuts

DIRECTIONS

1. As the first step, peel the avocado and remove the stone and the pulp.
2. After having removed the pulp, wash and dry it and then slice thinly.
3. Peel, wash, and dry the kiwi too, then cut it into little pieces.
4. Put the avocado, kiwi pieces, chopped hazelnuts, and vegetable milk in the glass of the blender, and blend all the ingredients at high speed.
5. Now add the ice and continue blending until you get a smooth and creamy mixture.
6. Once ready, turn off, stir with a wooden spoon, and pour the fruit and hazelnut smoothie into 2 glasses and serve.

68. Mango and Melon Smoothie

PREPARATION TIME: 5 minutes

CALORIES: 140

NUTRITIONAL VALUES: CARBS: 22 G; PROTEIN: 2 G; FAT: 3 G

INGREDIENTS FOR 2 SERVINGS

- 1 ripe mango
- 2.3 oz yellow melon pulp
- 2 tbsp sugar-free orange juice
- ½ cup sugar-free almond milk
- 2 tsp honey

DIRECTIONS

1. First, peel and wash the yellow melon pulp, then cut it into pieces.
2. Peel and slice the mango too, pit it then cut it into little pieces.
3. Put both mango and yellow melon pieces in a blender.
4. Add orange juice, 2 tsp honey, and almond milk.
5. Turn on the blender to obtain a smooth and homogeneous mixture.
6. Once reached the right consistency, pour the anti-inflammatory smoothie into 2 glasses and serve.

Dessert Recipes

69. Cinnamon, Cumin, and Coconut Baked Apples

PREPARATION TIME: 8 minutes

COOKING TIME: 10–12 minutes

CALORIES: 100

NUTRITIONAL VALUES: CARBS: 18 G; PROTEIN: 1 G; FAT: 2 G

INGREDIENTS

- 2 green apples
- 2 tsp olive oil
- ¼ tsp cumin powder
- 2 tsp honey
- ¼ tsp ground cinnamon
- 2 tbsp coconut flour

DIRECTIONS

1. Start this recipe by preheating the oven to 338°F.

2. Then, brush a baking pan with a bit of oil.

3. Meanwhile, peel and wash the 2 green apples and remove all the seeds.

4. Next, cut the apples into little cubes.

5. Now, combine the apple cubes with olive oil in a bowl.

6. Add ground cinnamon, cumin powder, coconut flour, and honey to the apple cubes, stirring until all ingredients are well combined.

7. Pour onto the baking pan and bake the apples for at least 20 minutes.

8. Serve these delicious apple cubes still hot.

70. Peach, Ginger, and Orange Ice Cream

PREPARATION TIME: 15 minutes

CALORIES: 160

NUTRITIONAL VALUES: CARBS: 28 G; PROTEIN: 6 G; FAT: 3 G

INGREDIENTS FOR 2 SERVINGS

- 5 oz ripe peach
- Juice of ½ blood orange
- 1 tsp powdered ginger
- 1 cup sugar-free soy milk
- 2 tsp honey

DIRECTIONS

1. First, peel, pit, and cut the peach into pieces that you will later transfer to the blender glass.

2. Add the soy milk and blend on medium speed until smooth and creamy.

3. Add honey, ginger, and blood orange juice.

4. Continue blending for 1 more minute.

5. Once well blended, pour the mixture into a container and take it to the freezer for at least 1 hour.

6. After 1 hour, place the mixture in an ice cream maker.

7. Turn on the machine and let it run for the indicated times.

8. Once ready, put the peach-ginger ice cream back in the freezer. Let it harden for the necessary time, and serve.

Meal Plan

Day 1

Breakfast: 1 omelet and 1 glass of citrus juice

Snack: 2 pears

Lunch: 7 oz of salmon, 7 oz of vegetables, and 1.7 oz of rye bread

Snack: 1 oz of extra dark chocolate

Dinner: 5.2 oz of chicken, 7 oz of vegetables, 1.7 oz of rye bread

Day 2

Breakfast: 1 pancake with protein flour, 1 cup of green tea

Snack: 1 smoothie

Lunch: 3.5 oz of legumes soup, 4.2 oz of turkey

Snack: 3.5 oz of Greek yogurt and 3.5 oz of blueberries

Dinner: 7 oz of cod, 7 oz of vegetables, 1.7 oz of whole grain bread

Day 3

Breakfast: 3.5 oz of Greek yogurt, rolled oats, kiwis, and 3 walnuts

Snack: 1 apple, 2 wholemeal rusks

Lunch: 2 oz of black rice, 5.2 oz of halibut, 5.2 oz of vegetables

Snack: 1 smoothie

Dinner: 5.2 oz of turkey, 7 oz of vegetables, 1.7 oz of oat bread

Day 4

Breakfast: 1 glass of pomegranate juice, 1 slice of wholemeal bread, 3 almonds

Snack: 3.5 oz of fruit salad

Lunch: 7 oz of tuna, 7 oz of vegetables, 1.7 oz of brown rice

Snack: 2 apricots

Dinner: 5.2 oz of chicken, 3.5 oz of legumes

Day 5

Breakfast: Kefir and porridge with oat flakes, blueberries, and chia seeds

Snack: 3.5 oz of strawberries, 1 whole grain rusk

Lunch: 7 oz of anchovies, 7 oz of vegetables, 1.7 oz of black rice

Snack: 3.5 oz of low-fat yogurt, 5 almonds

Dinner: 5.2 oz of chicken, 7 oz of vegetables, 1.7 oz of whole grain bread

Day 6

Breakfast: 1 cup of green tea, 1 protein yogurt, 1 pear

Snack: 3.5 oz of fruit salad

Lunch: 5.2 oz of turkey, 7 oz of vegetables, 1.7 oz of whole grain bread

Snack: 1 pear, 5 walnuts

Dinner: 7 oz of salmon, 7 oz of vegetables, and 1.7 oz of brown rice

Day 7

Breakfast: 1 omelet with spinach and turmeric, 3.5 oz of blackberries

Snack: 1 smoothie

Lunch: 3.5 oz of legumes soup, 4.2 oz of turkey

Snack: 2 little peaches

Dinner: 7 oz of cod, 7 oz of vegetables, 1.7 oz of whole grain bread

Day 8

Breakfast: 2 scrambled eggs, 1 glass of orange juice

Snack: 3.5 oz of kiwis, 2 almonds

Lunch: 7 oz of sardines, 7 oz of vegetables, 1.7 oz of whole grain bread

Snack: 3.5 oz of pineapple, 3 pistachios

Dinner: 5.2 oz of turkey, 7 oz of vegetables, 1.7 oz of whole grain bread

Day 9

Breakfast: 3.5 oz of protein yogurt, 3.5 oz of raspberries

Snack: 3.5 oz of cherries

Lunch: 7 oz of shrimp, 7 oz of vegetables, 1.7 oz of rye bread

Snack: 1 smoothie

Dinner: 7 oz of cod, 7 oz of vegetables, 1.7 oz of black rice

Day 10

Breakfast: 1 omelet and 1 glass of citrus juice

Snack: 1 smoothie

Lunch: 5.2 oz of chicken, 7 oz of vegetables, 1.7 oz of whole grain bread

Snack: 1 fruit salad

Dinner: 3.5 oz of legumes soup, 4.2 oz of turkey, 3.5 oz of vegetables

Day 11

Breakfast: 2 scrambled eggs, 1 glass of pomegranate juice

Snack: 3.5 oz of berries, 5 almonds

Lunch: 7 oz of salmon, 7 oz of vegetables, and 1.7 oz of rye bread

Snack: 1 oz of extra dark chocolate

Dinner: 7 oz of tilapia, 7 oz of vegetables, and 1.7 oz of brown rice

Day 12

Breakfast: 1 omelet with mushrooms, 3.5 oz of blueberries

Snack: 1 banana

Lunch: 7 oz of hake, 7 oz of vegetables, and 1.7 oz of whole grain bread

Snack: 1 smoothie

Dinner: 5.2 oz of chicken, 7 oz of vegetables, 1.7 oz of black rice

Day 13

Breakfast: 3.5 oz of Greek yogurt, rolled oats, ½ avocado, and 3 walnuts

Snack: 3.5 oz of cherries

Lunch: 7 oz of halibut, 7 oz of vegetables, and 1.7 oz of wholemeal pasta

Snack: 1 oz of extra dark chocolate

Dinner: 3.5 oz of legumes soup, 4.2 oz of chicken, 3.5 oz of vegetables

Day 14

Breakfast: 1 omelet and 1 glass of citrus juice

Snack: 3.5 oz of berries, 1 wholemeal biscuit

Lunch: 5.2 oz of chicken, 7 oz of vegetables, 1.7 oz of wholemeal pasta

Snack: ½ avocado, 5 strawberries

Dinner: 7 oz of halibut, 7 oz of vegetables, and 1.7 oz of rye bread

Day 15

Breakfast: 1 glass of pineapple juice, 1 slice of wholemeal bread, 3 almonds

Snack: 1 cup of green tea, 3.5 oz of peaches

Lunch: 5.2 oz of turkey, 7 oz of salad, 1.7 oz of rye bread

Snack: 1 banana, 3 almond

Dinner: 7 oz of shrimp, 7 oz of green salad, 1.7 oz of brown rice

Day 16

Breakfast: 1 pancake with protein flour, 1 cup of green tea

Snack: 1 smoothie

Lunch: 3.5 oz of legume soup, 5.2 oz of anchovies, 3.5 oz salad

Snack: 1 banana

Dinner: 5.2 oz of turkey, 7 oz of vegetables, 1.7 oz of gluten-free bread

Day 17

Breakfast: 1 pancake with protein flour, 1 cup of sugar-free almond milk

Snack: 1 glass of orange juice, 1 wholemeal rusk

Lunch: 3.5 oz of legumes soup, 4.2 oz of turkey, 3.5 oz of vegetables

Snack: 3.5 oz of pineapple

Dinner: 7 oz of mussels, 7 oz of vegetables, 1.7 oz of wholemeal pasta

Day 18

Breakfast: 2 scrambled eggs, ½ avocado, 1 tomato

Snack: 3.5 oz of berries, 5 almonds

Lunch: 7 oz of salmon, 7 oz of vegetables, and 1.7 oz of rye bread

Snack: 1 smoothie

Dinner: 5.2 oz of chicken, 7 oz of grilled vegetables, 1.7 oz of brown rice

Day 19

Breakfast: 1 omelet with spinach and turmeric, 3.5 oz of avocado

Snack: 3.5 oz of strawberries, 1 whole grain rusk

Lunch: 1 vegetable soup, 7 oz of anchovies, 1.7 oz of whole grain bread

Snack: 1 oz of extra dark chocolate

Dinner: 7 oz of cod, 7 oz of mixed salad, 1.7 oz of wholemeal pasta

Day 20

Breakfast: 3.5 oz of Greek yogurt, rolled oats, 5 strawberries, and 3 walnuts

Snack: 2 pears

Lunch: 7 oz of shrimp, 7 oz of green beans, 1.7 oz of rye bread

Snack: 1 cup of green tea, 3.5 oz of berries, 2 walnuts

Dinner: 3.5 oz of legumes, 7 oz of vegetables, 3.5 oz of salmon

Day 21

Breakfast: 2 scrambled eggs, 1 cup of sugar-free almond milk, 5 cherries

Snack: 3.5 oz of apples

Lunch: 7 oz of tuna, 1.7 oz of rye bread, 7 oz of grilled peppers

Snack: 1 smoothie

Dinner: 5.2 oz of turkey, 1.7 oz of black rice, 7 oz of mixed salad

Day 22

Breakfast: 1 pancake with protein flour, 1 cup of soy milk

Snack: 3.5 oz of strawberries, 5 almonds

Lunch: 1 vegetable soup, 1.7 oz of brown rice, 5.2 oz of cod

Snack: 3.5 oz of Greek yogurt, 5 cherries

Dinner: 7 oz of shrimp, 7 oz of green salad, 1.7 oz of brown rice

Day 23

Breakfast: 1 omelet with avocado and cherry tomatoes, 3.5 oz of blackberries

Snack: 3.5 oz of pineapple

Lunch: 7 oz of halibut, 7 oz of green beans, 1.7 oz of rye bread

Snack: 3.5 oz of peach, 1 wholegrain biscuit

Dinner: 5.2 oz of turkey, 7 oz of vegetables, 1.7 oz of gluten-free bread

Day 24

Breakfast: 3.5 oz of Greek yogurt, rolled oats, 1 tangerine, and 3 walnuts

Snack: 1 banana, 3 pistachios

Lunch: 5.2 oz of chicken, 7 oz of vegetables, 1.7 oz of whole grain bread

Snack: 3.5 oz of fruit salad with 2 tbsp of Greek yogurt

Dinner: 3.5 oz of legumes soup, 4.2 oz of turkey, 3.5 oz of vegetables

Day 25

Breakfast: 2 scrambled eggs, 1 glass of orange juice, 3 pistachios

Snack: 2 pears

Lunch: 7 oz of salmon, 7 oz of vegetables, and 1.7 oz of rye bread

Snack: 3.5 oz of pineapple, 1 wholemeal rusk

Dinner: 3.5 oz of legumes soup, 4.2 oz of turkey, 3.5 oz of vegetables

Day 26

Breakfast: 1 cup of green tea, 1 protein yogurt, 1 banana

Snack: 1 smoothie

Lunch: 3.5 oz of legumes soup, 4.2 oz of turkey, 3.5 oz of vegetables

Snack: 1 oz of dark chocolate

Dinner: 7 oz of halibut, 7 oz of vegetables, and 1.7 oz of rye bread

Day 27

Breakfast: 1 omelet, 3.5 oz of raspberries, 3 pecans

Snack: ½ avocado, 3 strawberries

Lunch: 7 oz of tilapia, 7 oz of vegetables, and 1.7 oz of brown rice

Snack: 2 peaches

Dinner: 7 oz of mussels, 7 oz of vegetables, 1.7 oz of wholemeal pasta

Day 28

Breakfast: 1 pancake with protein flour, 1 cup of green tea

Snack: 2 apricots, 3 walnuts

Lunch: 3.5 oz of legumes soup, 4.2 oz of turkey, 3.5 oz of vegetables

Snack: 2 kiwis, 5 almonds

Dinner: 3.5 oz of legumes, 7 oz of vegetables, 3.5 oz of salmon

Shopping List

Meat	Spices and aromatic herbs	Fruits
Chicken, turkey	Cinnamon, vanilla extract, jalapeno, cumin, ginger powder, turmeric powder, nutmeg, chili powder, curry powder, garam masala powder, pink peppercorn, chipotle, amchoor powder	Apricots, avocado, banana, kiwi, mango, orange, papaya, cherries, raspberries, lemon, pink grapefruits, lime, green olives, black olives, peaches, pineapple, pomegranate, plums, yellow melon, pears
Probiotics and milk substitutes Low-fat yogurt, sugar-free soy milk, sugar-free almond milk, sugar-free oat milk, coconut milk, soy cheese, low-fat white yogurt, tofu	**Sweeteners** Honey, extra dark chocolate	**Dried Fruits** Pistachios, strawberries, almond flakes, chopped cashews, pine nuts, pecans, hazelnuts
Cereals Wholemeal bread, wholemeal sandwich bread, wholemeal pasta, brown rice, quinoa, oat flakes	**Eggs**	**Vegetables** Cabbage, cucumber, beetroot, lettuce, carrots, scallions, garlic, squash, pumpkin, zucchini, tomatoes, asparagus, leeks, spring onion, onion, kale, yellow pepper, green pepper, turnips, broccoli, cherry tomatoes, mushrooms, spinach, radicchio
Flours Coconut flour, oat flour, wholemeal flour	**Herbs** Rosemary, bay leaves, dill, mint, chives, cilantro, parsley, sage, basil, thyme, coriander	**Seeds** Chia seeds, cardamom seeds, fenugreek seeds, mustard seeds
Legumes Peas, broad beans, chickpeas	**Fish** Scallops, tuna, plaice, smoked salmon, tilapia, trout, halibut, Alaska Pollock, hake	**Condiments** Apple cider vinegar, soy sauce, mustard

Printed in Great Britain
by Amazon

23132855R00057